Not By Strength
By Guile

+44 7775 151628

Not By Strength By Guile

PETER MERCER

BLAKE

Published by Blake Publishing Ltd,
3 Bramber Court, 2 Bramber Road,
London W14 9PB, England

First published in paperback in 2001

ISBN 1 85782 471 7

British Library Cataloguing-in-Publication Data:

A catalogue record for this book is
available from the British Library.

Typeset by t2

Printed and bound in Great Britain by
Bookmarque Ltd, Croydon, Surrey

3 5 7 9 10 8 6 4 2

Papers used by Blake Publishing Limited are natural,
recyclable products made from wood grown in sustain-
able forests. The manufacturing processes conform to the
environmental regulations of the country of origin.

Author's note

The modern Special Boat Service has emerged from a number of famous groups formed during World War II. The Army formed Special Boat Sections of 8 Commando in 1940; the Royal Marines Boom Patrol Detachment formed the famous Cockleshell Heroes unit in 1942; and the Royal Navy formed Combined Operations Pilotage Parties also in 1942. After the war, the Special Boat Section was re-formed under the Royal Marines and later the title was changed to Special Boat Squadron. Today, the official title has become the Special Boat Service.

In order to protect the identity of my colleagues in the Special Forces and elsewhere, certain names have been changed.

Peter Mercer

CONTENTS

GLOSSARY

ASU	Active Service Unit
AWOL	absent without leave
CO	Commanding Officer
COPP	Combined Operations Pilotage Party
GPMG	General Purpose Machine-Gun
HE	high explosives
LZ	landing zone
MCT	Marine Counter-Terrorism
MPA	Maritime Patrol Aircraft
MTB	motor torpedo boat
The Net	communications network
OP	observation post
PJI	Parachute Jump Instructor
RAOC	Royal Army Ordnance Corps
REME	Royal Electrical and Mechanical Engineers
RIB	ribbed inflatable boat
RPG	rocket-propelled grenade
RV	rendezvous
sangar	security post
Sarbies	search and rescue beacon
SBS	Special Boat Service
SDV	swimmer delivery vehicle
VCP	vehicle check-point

To my parents and the friends and family who
have stood by me

CHAPTER ONE

For eight long, hot hours under a scorching sun, we had been out on the road patrolling the hills and dry dirt valleys some twenty miles from our base camp in northern Iraq. My mouth was dry, my tongue swollen, lips caked with dust and dirt; sweat dripped from my forehead into my eyes, and my shirt and trousers were black with perspiration and grime. The desert, the hills, the valleys surrounding us shimmered in the heat and the vehicles rumbled towards us, slowly emerging from the haze, the blazing sun reflecting like diamonds on the car roofs. All I wanted was rest and something for my thirst, but this was a long,

long day and I needed to ration the water. The gear on my back seemed to weigh a bloody ton.

Our 16-man patrol of 40 Commando had been tasked to cover around six square miles stretching towards the Kurdish encampments hidden in the mountain ranges above our Tactical Area of Responsibility. As the day continued to sap our lagging energy, the heat enveloping our tired bodies in lethargy, we spent the hours examining our watches, waiting patiently for the sun to go down, so we could make our way back to camp to rest, drink and enjoy a cold shower and some scran.

Then the 'net' — the communications network — crackled into life.

'Two motor vehicles are heading towards your position,' said the voice in a cool monotone. 'We need you to set up an ambush by a road-block. The occupants of the two vehicles are engaged in a fire-fight and they must be stopped at all costs. Use minimum force.'

We all understood that the order to use 'minimum force' meant that we should only attempt to stop the vehicle by shooting out the tyres and the engine, rather than take out the driver, the occupants and the whole bloody car.

'Shit,' said one of the patrol, 'let's go.'

Headquarters had given us no indication of the vehicles or the identities of the men involved in the fire-fight. And we had no idea how well they were armed or, indeed, what weapons they were carrying. We split up, two men standing by the improvised road-block, four men behind cover on both sides of the road and the remaining two Royal Marines acting as cut-off some yards down the road towards base camp. We were all dressed in camouflage fatigues and armed with SA80s and two light support weapons with bipod legs.

Fifteen minutes later, as we waited anxiously, our fingers on the safety catches, the net crackled into life again.

'The car you must stop is a white Peugeot.'

Nothing else. No further information. We all watched the bend in the road about 200 yards away, waiting for the white Peugeot to appear, wondering whether the car contained members of Saddam Hussein's crack Presidential Guard or the rebel force.

Suddenly, the Peugeot rounded the bend and came careering down the road at about 60mph towards the two Marine Commandos waiting by the road block. They put up their hands indicating to the driver to stop but he took no notice. As the Peugeot accelerated towards the two Commandos, the men in the car opened fire, spraying their AK-47s at the two sentries. The driver obviously had no intention of stopping. I was one of the four men in the second line of defence and when we saw what was happening we just opened up, firing at the tyres and the engine. Within seconds, the tyres had been cut to ribbons and the car was forced to a halt. We continued to pour rounds into the engine to ensure that the car could not take off again. But the stupid bastards inside the vehicle continued to fire at us and so we returned fire.

Suddenly, the firing stopped. I wondered whether we had shot the drivers. I could see no one in the vehicle, not even the driver. We ran towards it, and then saw the occupants lying low inside the car. We grabbed their weapons, pulled them from the vehicle and threw them away. Then we opened the doors, grabbed the four men and hauled them out by the scruff of the neck, making sure they were lying face down. Two of us stood over them with our S80s aimed at their backs as two others frisked them to see if they had any other hidden weapons. They were clean. But we were taking no chances with men who, only a few seconds earlier, had tried to shoot our mates at the road block. Two of the occupants were wounded but we soon ascertained that neither wound was life threatening. We then went through their pockets in a more thorough search, looking for ID cards or driving licences, trying to discover any clue as to their nationality. We found nothing.

We called Headquarters and reported what had happened. We were ordered to remain, guard the men and await the arrival of the Military Police. The four men regarded us warily, glancing at our weapons, but didn't move a muscle. After a day in that desert sun, we must have looked mean and nasty. They sensed that and remained motionless.

Later, we heard that the four men were members of Saddam Hussein's Presidential Guard who had decided to desert and escape to Turkey. They knew that if any Iraqi soldiers had found them, they would all have been executed on the spot. But as they sped in their Peugeot towards the border, they had been spotted by Kurdish fighters of the PPK who had given chase. The fire-fight continued as the vehicles raced along the scorching tarmac road towards the Turkish border. Fearing that they would be taken out as the chasing PPK gunmen came closer, the Iraqi guards decided to make a fight of it.

Having rounded a bend, the Iraqi guards pulled off the road and hid behind some trees. Three leapt from their vehicle and took up positions waiting for the PPK. Twenty seconds later, the four PPK gunmen came hurtling along the road, to be met by a fusillade of bullets. The driver was killed instantly, a bullet through the head. Their car careered off the road and crashed into a rock. Before any of the PPK gunmen had time to react, the Iraqis raced to the vehicle and poured round after round into the occupants as they struggled to escape. Within seconds it was over. Without bothering to examine the men they had just murdered, the Iraqis ran back to their car to continue their desperate escape.

They were asked by Arabic-speaking British Intelligence officers why they hadn't stopped when ordered to do so by the British Commandos. The men replied that they had been warned by Saddam Hussein that if they ever surrendered to any Allied forces they would be summarily executed — shot by firing squad, without trial. They had chosen to try to fight their way through any Allied road block rather than face a firing squad.

Those four Iraqi guards never realised how lucky they had been coming across the Royal Marine Commandos, for many soldiers would have been tempted to take immediate action against such bastards after seeing the number of innocent kids who had been killed and maimed by the deliberate and despicable actions taken by the retreating Iraqi forces. They had left booby-traps everywhere. There were booby-traps in all the houses, attached to weapons and even toys, kettles and buckets, furniture and chairs, spades and machinery, as well as the detritus of smashed vehicles and artillery pieces.

We saw countless kids without hands, arms or feet, lost as a result of picking up booby-traps. Some of the booby-traps contained home-made explosives, others high explosives (HE) and some contained white phosphorous which burned the skin to a cinder. The results were truly horrific and we wondered how grown men could leave such traps for innocent young kids of whatever nationality. And, on occasions, as we patrolled along the metal roads, we would see numbers of children lying dead by the side of the road. Sometimes we would see only one or two bodies;

at other times perhaps the remains of ten or more young boys and girls, the oldest about ten or so, the youngest barely able to walk.

Some of those kids had died in road accidents and some had unfortunately been killed by Allied vehicles. As we sped from one spot to another in Iraq, we would be riding in 4-ton trucks travelling at speeds in excess of 50mph. Without fail, we would often come across groups of hungry Kurdish kids who would be attracted by the clouds of dust thrown up by the vehicles perhaps a mile or more distant. Then the kids would race towards the road and run along the sides of the speeding vehicles, their hands stretched out to the soldiers, begging for food. And many of the kids seemed oblivious to the dangers, often running in front of the vehicles in a vain bid to bring them to a halt. I must have witnessed half-a-dozen terrible accidents in which the driver would have to brake sharply and take evasive action in an unsuccessful attempt to avoid one or more children who had deliberately run out into the path of the truck to obtain food.

On one occasion I was in a 4-ton truck on our way back to base when we saw a group of around 30 or so kids running towards the road, screaming and shouting for food, their arms stretched out towards us. We couldn't stop because we would then have been a sitting target for Iraqi troops and we had no food for the children. When we reached them, they screamed at us, although they seemed to have learned their lesson and had left a wide path for the trucks to drive through. Our driver slowed, of course, but when it became obvious to the children that we were not going to stop, two girls simply walked out in front of us. The driver didn't stand a chance. He had only been driving at around 15mph, but before we had stopped, I realised we had hit them and they were beneath the vehicle. We jumped down as the mothers of the children came running towards us, yelling and screaming. While some of our lads tried to calm the women, I and three other mates crawled under the vehicle to see if there was anything we could do for the two girls. As soon as I saw them lying there, I knew they were dead. Of course, we went through the motions, took their pulses and examined them, but there was no response. We took them carefully from under the vehicle and placed them as gently as possible by the side of the road, covering their bodies with blankets. On the way back to base, no one spoke; we sat looking at our feet, fighting back the tears and wondering if there was any way that we could have spared the lives of those innocent children.

It seemed horribly ironic that 3 Commando Brigade had been sent to northern Iraq to help protect and guard the Kurdish people. They had fled to the north in a bid to save their skins when the defeated Saddam Hussein decided to vent his rage by attacking and slaughtering them after his humiliation at the hands of the UN forces. Now, it seemed, on the pretext of protection, we had inadvertently, yet unavoidably, added to their suffering.

Throughout Desert Storm, I and many of my mates in the Royal Marines had felt extremely frustrated and disappointed that throughout that campaign we had been forced to stay at home in Britain watching the nightly news of the campaign, rather than being asked to take an active part in a real war. I had frequently vented my frustration to the Provost-Sergeant at Poole in Dorset where, throughout the war, I had been stationed on guard duty at the Special Boat Service headquarters. It had just been plain bad luck that I was on that 18-month long, boring tour of duty at Poole: my name, like the others with me, had simply been drawn out of a hat. But it didn't help my anger and frustration. My Provost-Sergeant knew I was mightily pissed off and understood my feelings, although he thought I was mad wanting to go and fight in the desert.

During leave in April 1991, I was at home watching television when I heard the news that 3 Commando Brigade, including 40 Commando, 45 Commando and artillery and logistics, around 2,500 men altogether, had been ordered to the Gulf to take over from troops who had been out there for months. It was understood that they were to fly to northern Iraq to protect the Kurdish minority from the Iraqi forces. That night, I invited my girlfriend Sue, a great girl, to come and have a drink or three at my father's pub — The Reading House — near the beach at Cleveden, north Somerset. Together, we got really pissed. I was drowning my sorrows, and Sue, a bright, intelligent, attractive girl who worked in computer sales, was matching me pint for rough pint of glorious, cloudy, intoxicating cider.

The following morning, I awoke alone in Sue's bed with a thumping head to the sound of yelling and banging and I thought I could hear my father's voice calling my name. I stumbled out of bed and went to the window. He was standing in the middle of the road asking everyone who passed whether they could tell him which was the house of a girl named Sue.

'What do you want?' I shouted from the bedroom window.

'Oh, Pete,' shouted my father, 'your boss at Poole has been on the phone.'

'My boss?' I shouted back. 'Who do you mean?'

'Your Provost-Sergeant,' he said. 'He wants you to phone him at Poole ASAP.'

'Give me a minute,' I shouted. 'I'll see you at home.'

Within five minutes, I was speaking to my Provost-Sergeant.

'What do you want?' I asked.

'Listen,' he replied, 'do you still want to go to Iraq?'

'Fuck me, yes,' I said. 'Why?'

'Don't ask me how I did it,' he said, 'but I've put your name forward. I heard that 40 Commando need some more men to fly immediately to northern Iraq to help repatriate and guard the Kurds. Interested?'

'My God, yes,' I shouted.

'I've more good news for you,' he said. 'If that works out all right, you won't have to return to Poole for any further guard duty either.'

'Shit!' I screamed. 'Really?'

'Yes,' he said. 'Now get your arse down here ASAP and report to me. OK?'

'OK,' I said. 'See you.'

I threw my gear into a hold-all and took off for Poole in the old, dilapidated Opel Kadett bequeathed me by my grandfather. I had only been travelling an hour or so when the car suddenly ground to a halt. I didn't know what was wrong but decided to leave the vehicle in a lay-by and thumb a lift. Four hours later, I arrived at Poole. In fact, I would discover later that the Opel had simply run out of fuel but, because the gauge showed it to be half-full, I didn't know what was wrong.

Somewhat flustered and hassled that it had taken so long to report for duty, my heart missed a beat when I presented myself to the Provost-Sergeant to be told that there had been a change of plan.

'Oh, no,' I said, a gut-wrenching feeling in the pit of my stomach.

'You're no longer joining 40 Commando,' he said. 'They need men with your helicopter skills for the Royal Marines and the US Marines helicopter teams, so you're going with them.'

That made sense. I had been trained to call in choppers for day and night attacks, and to set up and secure the landing sites. The Provost-Sergeant, armed with the 'Troop Bible' — in which is detailed the different skills, qualifications and training schedules of every Royal Marine — had simply checked my listing and realised I possessed those skills.

'Great news,' I said, 'thanks a million. I just want to get out there. Any job's fine by me.'

'Now listen,' said the Provost-Sergeant. 'Get a travel warrant and take a train to Plymouth and report to the Commando Logistics Regiment. You'll be joining them and 600 or so other Marines.'

By the time I arrived in Plymouth some hours later, I had totally sobered up and was eager to join the action.

I phoned Sue and told her what was happening.

'Take care,' she said, 'and write whenever you can. Good luck.'

'Thanks,' I said, 'good luck. I'll be thinking of you.' It's difficult to know exactly what to say in those situations because you're all pumped-up, the adrenalin flowing, wanting to get out there and see some action. But you can't say that in those tender moments of farewell. You have to suppress your emotions, although all you really want to do is get on a plane and get stuck in.

Forty-eight hours later, the 800 men of the Logistics Regiment and 45 Commando were travelling by coach to Brize Norton to embark for Turkey. We had been informed by Military Intelligence that the weather in northern Iraq was freezing, several degrees below zero at night and, therefore, we'd been told to draw arctic and cold-weather equipment including skis, thermal underwear, white camouflage gear, and arctic tents and rations. The rations are basically dehydrated so that snow can be added and then the food is heated in the water when boiled on a little solid-block fuel stove.

We were all waiting in the car park at Brize Norton, packing our gear on to a 4-ton truck to transport everything to the waiting Hercules C-130 transport plane, when a Marine Sergeant-Major called for everyone's attention.

'Anyone here ever used one of these things?' he asked, pointing to bazooka-like launchers lying on the ground.

'What are they?' someone asked.

'They're called a Law Ninety,' he said. 'They're disposable, hand-held anti-tank missile launchers.'

I knew what they were, because I had only recently completed a course on learning how to fire them.

'Yes,' I piped up, 'I've just done a training course on them.'

'Right. Out here,' said the Sergeant-Major. 'Now, everyone gather round and listen to what you're being told. One day your life might depend on it.'

'How long have we got?' I asked.

'Maximum of two hours,' he replied.

Fortunately, there was a single dummy Law 90 and so I began my lecture, desperately trying to recall what I had been taught some weeks earlier. I taught them everything I knew and then invited as many Marines as possible to come out and go through the loading, firing and safety techniques, so at least some of them had some experience of handling the new weapon. In essence, the Law 90 was based on the old-fashioned hand-held bazooka, but was now much more powerful, accurate and devastating.

When the trigger is pulled, the Law 90 initially fires three 9mm rounds, fitted with flash tips, which light up if you've hit the target tank. If successful, the trigger is moved to main armament, a high-explosive armour-piercing round, and the missile should then be zeroed in on the bullet fired earlier. A tiny hole is pierced in the tank's armament, and then the rest of the high explosive is squirted into the tank and vaporises everything inside, including the metal, wireless, ammunition, equipment and the human bodies.

Ninety minutes later, the lecture was over and everyone had a rough knowledge of how to handle and fire the new launchers. On arrival in Turkey, I was given my new task, working as ground crew to locate and then protect suitable helicopter landing sites. Within 24 hours of disembarking, we had been given an intelligence briefing, various friendly and enemy locations on military maps and a weather report, telling us that our base in the mountains would be freezing. We took off in Chinooks and landed a few miles inside the Iraqi border. We were taking no chances. We were dropped in total darkness at 1.00am and ordered to fan out and secure the entire area. The enemy, we were told, was about 25 miles away and the US ground forces were expected to arrive in our area within 48 hours.

At 05.30 we stood to, watching for any enemy. We were in thermal underwear and basic artic kit, including artic windproof smocks and trousers. When we emerged from our nine-inch deep scrapes in the ground, the sun was rising into a bright blue, cloudless sky. Four hours later, the heat was unbearable; the temperature had risen to over 90° Fahrenheit and we were sweltering in our arctic gear. Someone had fucked up, big time. We stripped off everything except our smocks which we left open. We couldn't take off all our clothes because we had no sun block and I had to wear my arctic snow-blind goggles as sunglasses! We managed to protect ourselves using our ponchos as sun shelters, lying under them in the scorching heat of the midday sun. That first day, the valley where we were situated, some seven miles from the town of Silopi, was covered in wonderful green vegetation, but within a week or so it had all but disappeared, and given way to sandy-coloured rock, earth and crags.

Having set up our PRC–320 man-pack long-distance radio, which was capable of transmitting and receiving back to our HQ in Britain, we prepared an area for the arrival of our arsenal of four Apache helicopter gunships.

The following morning, I awoke to a thunderous noise which seemed to make the very earth tremble and wondered if we were in the middle of an earthquake. We slipped out of our scrapes in the ground to investigate and saw in the distance a massive convoy heading towards us, one which seemed to have no end. We saw tanks on scores of low-loaders, hundreds of huge trucks, refrigerated vehicles, water trucks, jeeps and choppers flying sorties in the distance in and out of the encampment area only a mile from our tiny enclave. For the following 36 hours, we watched in awe the arrival of the US Marines and the small town they seemed to have brought with them from somewhere in middle America. Then we decided to go and investigate to see how the other half lived.

'Gob-smacked' was the only word for what we witnessed that day. This little town, set up inside a wire perimeter fence, must have been three or more acres.

'How're you doing?' was the only question

the US Marine on guard duty asked when we showed up at the main gate. He didn't ask for any ID, or where we came from, and we simply walked in and took a look around. We understood this camp was only for the chopper pilots, gunners and air crew, the flight engineers and two recce platoons to guard the area. But this base also housed a fully-equipped field hospital, a cinema, a battery of telephone kiosks, a bank of showers with running hot and cold water, refrigerated trucks with water and provisions, a café serving excellent food, a Coke dispenser and a complete four-hour laundry service. We had our scrapes dug into the dirt, very little water for washing or shaving, no change of clothes, dehydrated rations and only powder for our feet, armpits and crotches!

As a result of finding this Shangri-la in the middle of the desert, we decided to enjoy it to the full. We began by asking US officers and senior NCO whether we could have some water, a meal or a drink and we always received the same reply, 'Help yourselves, be our guests, make yourselves at home.' And we did, happily making the three-mile hike each day to enjoy hot showers, good food and the occasional movie. But it would not always be like that.

CHAPTER TWO

The sea was calm that night, the tide high, and the moon shone from the cloudless skies, illuminating the spot on the beach where I stood looking out across the Bristol Channel towards Wales and, in my mind, to the magical adventures and excitement that the seas and the oceans would one day hold for me. As I gazed, spellbound, in the warm night air, my young mind played tricks and I imagined myself on one of the three large oil tankers that I could see ploughing their silent way along the Channel to some distant land. As I daydreamed, my attention was drawn to a small fleet of fishing smacks which bobbed into the shaft of moonlight, their lights playing hide and seek as they chugged out to sea and the fishing grounds where they would spend the night.

During my teenage years, I would spend hours walking up and down that stretch of shingle gazing out to the horizon, forever throwing pebbles across the water. I would come here to think and wonder and plan my future. This beach had captured my imagination from the moment I first made my way from my parents' home in nearby Clevedon, a small West Country town in the estuary between Bristol and the seaside town of Weston-super-Mare. To me, a young lad of 12, the beach was always vast and glimmering, the sea cold and threatening in the dark of winter but warm and welcoming in the summer months. Whenever the winds blew hard, I would cycle down to the beach to watch and listen to the roar of the waves and the delicate noise of the shingle as the tide tugged the millions of tiny pebbles against their wishes, enveloping them in its power. The ebb and flow fascinated and surprised me, but it was the power of the ocean that caught my imagination. Even then I was convinced that the seas would give me a life of dreams and adventure and I wondered whether that life would be one of peace and happiness or of danger and pain, embroiled in a perpetual struggle like the sea itself.

My father was a former policeman, my mother a dancer and we lived with my baby sister Sarah in York before moving to Welwyn Garden City near London when I was just six. At the age of 12, my life changed dramatically when we moved to Clevedon in Somerset and my father joined Courage breweries. Our lovely four-bedroom detached house was only two miles from the Bristol Channel and surrounded by woodland. No boy could have grown up in more wonderful natural surroundings, with the woods and the coastline to explore.

My passion for sport would eventually bear fruit, too, but not for some years. I loved rugby and athletics and was considered a natural. As a consequence, I trained and practised and played my heart out, developing my physique, strength and stamina. I was also selected to represent my school, town and, occasionally, the county and I loved in the challenge of competitive sport. At the age of 15, however, my father decided to buy a pub of his own and I found myself living a strange existence, attending school by day and enjoying living in a good, old-fashioned, friendly pub, and making friends with many of the regulars. I also learned how to play a fair game of pool, too.

I was, in fact, enjoying life too much and, as a result, my school work suffered. I was 16, thought I knew it all and decided I wanted to leave. Quite rightly, of course, my parents tried to persuade me to stay on, take my GCSE exams, and then make a decision. But I was 16 and stubborn and began playing truant. I preferred riding my motor-bike, dare-devil fashion, anywhere and everywhere, and within a few months had nearly got myself killed. A few weeks later my parents relented, allowing me to quit school, and I immediately found a job in a cobbler's, repairing shoes. During those first few weeks, I felt so important and, earning £48 a week, quite rich, too. But I quickly tired of that job as I imagined my entire life stuck behind a counter repairing smelly shoes. So I looked around for something else to fire my imagination. I found a better job making windows and, at the same time, doubled my income. And a few months before my seventeenth birthday, I decided I wanted my independence and I moved out of the pub to share a house with a mate. Life seemed idyllic; I was my own boss, I had drinks every night, parties every weekend, dances on a Saturday night and hangovers every morning. But within months, I had come to realise that this was not the life for me.

One day, I went for a training run and found myself puffing and wheezing. Twelve months before I had been the schools' cross-country champion with a six-pack stomach, and in less than a year I had become a pale shadow of the young man I was; pathetic, unfit, drinking too much, working at a boring, dead-end job and pissing away my pay every night. I knew in that instant that my life had to change so I went down to the job centre.

'Join The Army' urged the large poster in front of me. As my mate Marcus wandered around the centre also looking for a job, I began to think of joining the Army. I had never thought for one moment of making a career of the Army; it had never even crossed my mind. And when I told Marcus that's what I intended to do, he simply laughed out loud and bet me I would never do it.

The next day, we walked into the Bristol recruiting centre.

'What can I do for you two?' were the words that greeted us, spoken by a Sergeant in a well-pressed uniform and sporting a wonderful walrus moustache.

'For him, nothing,' I replied cheekily, 'but I want to join the Army.'

'Right, come this way then,' he said. 'You can go,' he added to Marcus.

'He's my lift,' I said in an appealing voice. 'Can't he stay?'

'You won't have anyone to hold your hand in the Army,' the Sergeant snapped. 'Are you a mummy's boy or something?'

I remained silent but it appeared that the Sergeant had hit upon his favourite subject. He prattled on about the youth of today being soft and pathetic and Marcus began to laugh. 'What the fuck are you laughing at, you little shit?' shouted the Sergeant, turning puce.

I thought this abuse must be some psychological test one had to pass before being accepted into the Army, but I just didn't like the stream of sarcasm and insults that the Sergeant was now using in an effort to belittle us.

'You can piss off,' I said, and Marcus and I turned and began to walk out of the building.

As we walked out, I saw another soldier standing across the corridor, laughing at the situation. He was tall, muscular, quite young and he seemed pretty hard, even menacing. I thought we were going to have to fight our way out of the recruiting office.

'You decided not to join the Army, then?' he asked laughing.

'No,' I replied, 'that bloke had a right attitude.'

'Why don't you come in here then and take a look?' he asked.

'No thanks,' I replied, 'that's the end of my army career.'

'We're not the Army,' he said reassuringly. 'Come and take a look. I'll make you a wet.'

Before I realised what was happening, I followed him into his office, wondering what the hell a 'wet' was. I had never heard of one before.

Marcus grabbed my arm. 'These guys are the fucking Marines,' he whispered, 'Marine Commandos.'

The officer gave me a cup of tea and we sat and listened to his patter, but as he spoke I knew I had not the slightest intention of joining a mob like the Marines. That was way too tough for me. But I did listen.

'We're not the Army. From us you'll get firm, fair orders and instructions. But you do have to be tough. The training is the hardest, longest and toughest in Europe and if you don't come up to scratch, if you can't take it, you're out. What we do is point you in the right direction, tell you what to do and then the rest is up to you.'

The more he talked, the more I began to warm to the idea. I had always been fit, strong and healthy, one of the most athletic lads at school. Then he asked me to step up to the pull-up bar and do some exercises. 'Great,' I thought, 'now I'll show him, I can do loads of these.'

But I was badly out of shape and I hadn't fully realised it. I did a pathetic five and had to stop, feeling embarrassed and somewhat shamefaced.

'All right,' he said, 'that's OK,' and I had to look at him twice because I knew five was bloody useless. He told me to take away some forms, fill them in and get them signed by my parents, because I was not yet 18, and return the following week for a full medical.

My parents hardly said a word when I told them of my plans to join the Marines and they happily signed the papers. I fancied my father believed this was simply my latest hair-brained idea which would start with razzmatazz and a bang and end soon enough in ignominy. But I returned the following week with my papers and was surprised when the doctor passed me A1. A week later I had returned once more and, along with nine other would-be recruits, sat down to complete a written exam. Because I had left school at the age of 16, I was worried I would fail but, surprisingly, I was one of the few to pass and the Marine Captain told me to go home, start circuit training and concentrate on hard, steep hill runs.

The letter from the Ministry of Defence arrived seven days later and contained a return rail ticket to Lympstone in Devon, a village on the River Exe, a few miles north of Exmouth. The instructions were brief and to the point telling me to take my PE kit, wash gear and clean, smart civilian clothes, in order to attend a three-day Potential Recruits Course, the physical aptitude test for the Royal Marines. Fifteen of us assembled at Lympstone railway station to be greeted by a Marine dressed immaculately and wearing boots you could see your face in. As we were marched off to the barracks, I feared I was making a terrible mistake, especially when I saw the World War II-type hut and the bunks we would have to sleep in. My mate on the bunk below was a huge, powerfully built, odd-looking bloke who worked as a grave-digger and looked like one!

The boots — manky, old things — the green overalls and heavy green jacket had all seen better days and as I clambered into my rock-hard bunk that night I realised the Marines was not for me. I was also pretty certain that I didn't have a cat-in-hell's chance of passing the course. I was just drifting off to sleep when there was a noise at the door and the lights were switched on.

'Right, time to get up,' shouted the Marine waking us. 'It's five-thirty; breakfast is at six sharp. Have a shit, shower and shave and be lined up outside at five-fifty in time for breakfast. Now get a move on.'

We ate a quick breakfast, returned to our hut and changed into PE strip for the first training exercise of the day. As we stood waiting outside the hut at 6.30am it was still dark; dawn had yet to break. At the double, we ran to the gym and were met by two PTIs (Physical Training Instructors) and told what was to happen. After warming up, we had to undergo a system of exercises called the USMC (United States Marine Corps) tests. These were designed to check the entry level of recruits to the US Marines. For the Royal Marines these were tests just to see if we had a basic level of fitness simply to start training. Thirty minutes later I was shattered, hardly able to breathe or move but I had completed 68 press-ups and 85 sit-ups, all under the eagle-eye of a PTI. And that was simply the warm-up routine! 'Fuck,' I thought to myself, 'I'll never last three days.'

A few of us asked to go outside to be sick and after that little break it was a four-mile run behind a slow-moving Land Rover. Five of the lads dropped out. Back at the camp we had to tackle the assault course which had to be completed in five minutes. I went off like a bat out of hell but had to stop half-way round to be sick again. But I did manage 4 mins and 11 seconds, although half of the recruits failed.

The Sergeant told us, 'Well done those who passed, tough shit on those who failed. For your information, during training this will have to be completed in five minutes in full combat gear weighing 24lb and with an 11lb weapon as well.' I felt like packing in the whole idea of being a Marine. In fact, after tea that evening, five of the lads did jack in the course, packed their bags and went off to the railway station and home.

In a way, their departure made me feel better, giving me the confidence to stay the rest of the course despite feeling wretched and exhausted. When I awoke the following morning I could hardly move; pain gripped my thighs, calves and arm muscles; my back muscles also hurt like shit. I wondered if undertaking this physical test had been a good idea. But, deep down, I wanted to continue, to prove myself, to show my dad that I could take whatever was thrown at me. The early morning start on the second day was in the swimming pool and the first test was to dive off the top board. But the swimming did seem to relax the muscles in time for the afternoon physical test — the endurance course, undertaken in our boots and overalls. Most of the afternoon was spent crawling through water-filled tunnels, running across miles of rain-soaked tracks and then wading through streams and pools with the water at chin level. The course ended with another heart-pounding run keeping up with the Land Rover. Some, of course, didn't make it, but those who did clambered silent and exhausted into the back of the 4-tonner which had brought us from camp, the steam from our hot, sweaty bodies drifting upwards in the cold air.

In the showers the following morning, we all burst out laughing as we realised we were all walking around, moaning rather like a group of grumpy pensioners who wanted to crawl back to bed and sleep the day away. But judgement hour was fast approaching and we were all lined up outside the Company Sergeant-Major's office to hear who had passed. The Sergeant-Major ordered half a dozen of us into the office, having dismissed the others.

'Right,' he said, glaring at each of us in turn, 'against my better judgement I've decided in my usual Godly generosity that you sorry lot will be allowed to start training as future Royal Marines. Now, attention! Right turn! Now pat the bloke in front of you on the back and tell him "well done".'

His sense of humour did, however, break the ice and everyone smiled and said 'well done'. I had to admit to a wonderful sense of euphoria, an enormous feeling of achievement. And I couldn't wipe the smile from my face as I took the train back to Clevedon and to my parents. I downed a pint of beer and then went upstairs to change while my mother cooked me a meal. I never ate the meal. I awoke 36 hours later after the longest, deepest sleep of my life.

Three months later, in February 1989, I once again set off for Lympstone which I sensed was almost the Royal Marines' own private hamlet in Devon. I knew that ahead of me lay eight months of the toughest, longest basic training of any of the NATO forces, and that included the Americans. Part of me was looking forward to the challenge; the other part felt like getting back on the train, heading home and forgetting the whole damn idea. But something refused to let me take the coward's way out. I felt this training was something I had to do, perhaps to prove to myself once and for all that I could live with the hardest, toughest lads in the world and survive with a smile on my face.

The induction phase lasted two weeks which, after being given our kit, began at the barber's where we were unceremonially scalped. As I walked out of the barber's shop five minutes later, I suddenly realised that the die was cast. I had no option but to stay and go through with the basic training for I could never go home looking like a skinhead!

The discipline was extreme and there was no room whatsoever for error. From the very first day, the effect on body, arms and legs was numbing and within days I knew I was struggling to keep up. Every day I felt like quitting but something kept urging me to stay and prove myself. I knew I wanted to be in the Royal Marines but I understood that the Marines didn't need me. If I didn't — or rather, couldn't — make the grade, I was out. People were leaving or being told to leave every week, but somehow I managed, just, to hang in there.

Towards the end of the 15 weeks' training, I was called to a meeting in the troop's training team office. As I stood to attention waiting to hear the worst, my Troop Sergeant gave it to me straight.

'Right, Mercer,' he said, 'I won't beat about the bush. You're borderline, son. Your admin is just about acceptable, field craft OK and your physical training is about average. We're starting commando training shortly which will make what you're doing now seem like a walk in the park. You really need to get your shit together or you'll get into difficulties. However, I think you have the determination to get through, but only if you pull your finger out. Understand?'

'Yes, Sergeant,' I replied.

'Right. About turn and get lost,' said the Sergeant, 'and sort your shit out.'

I survived the 15-week course and my parents came for the pass-out parade, bringing my beautiful girlfriend Heather with them. We performed some gymnasium displays and tackled the assault course to give them a brief insight into what we had been doing over the previous four months. Then it was our first weekend pass and I went home to celebrate, managing, of course, to get blind drunk.

I arrived back at camp on the Monday morning still suffering from a thumping headache and the first order was to parade in full fighting kit, carrying a weapon. For the first time we were tackling the assault course in full kit. Somehow, I completed the course in three minutes, forty seconds, the fastest in the troop. That one, single achievement convinced me that I could stick the eight-month course as long as I continued to put my mind to it. The training, however, became more intense, the pressure greater, the physical effort more demanding and we were also learning basic military skills, weapons training, signals, unarmed combat and drill. And we were allowed to go into Lympstone for a drink on Saturday nights. It wasn't long before trouble followed.

One night, a mate and I were sitting at a table in the Turks Head having a pint or two when two local girls came up to chat. My mate and one of the girls went off together and I was just explaining to the other girl that I had a steady back home when I suddenly felt a sickening pain at the base of my skull. The girl screamed as I spun round and saw three men standing before me, one with a broken bottle in his hand. Apparently, one of them was this girl's ex-boyfriend and he was the jealous type. I put my hand to my head and it felt wet. When I checked, my hand was covered in blood.

'Look, mate,' I said, trying to calm the situation, 'I was only talking to her; it's totally innocent.'

'Fuck you,' said one, 'no one fools around with my girl.'

I feared the worst so I decided to take the initiative and launched myself at the lad holding the broken bottle. I must have got in three or four really powerful punches before I went down in a torrent of blows to the head. The rest was just a haze but I took a really bad pasting that night. The three men left me lying almost unconscious and fled. I sustained a fractured cheek bone, broken teeth and massive bruising to the body where they had kicked the hell out of me after knocking me to the ground. Somehow, I managed to get back to camp and was taken to the sick bay where my head was stitched and my other wounds bathed.

After three days in the sick bay, the Medical Officer put me on 'light duty' orders for a week. I was told to report the incident to the police and did so, telling them that I could not remember what my attackers looked like. A week or so later, I was fully recovered.

A month later, I was back in town having a drink with some mates when the same girl came up to me apologising for what had happened. Within a minute or so, her former boyfriend walked in and caught us chatting together so, not wanting any more trouble, I finished my pint and walked outside. Minutes later, the boyfriend, accompanied by his two mates, followed.

'We told you to stay away,' one said cockily. 'Haven't you fucking had enough?'

'Look, dickhead,' I replied, 'I don't know what's wrong with you but I don't want any trouble.'

The three men began to walk menacingly towards me and I was just about to take one of them out when the pub door opened and two of my mates emerged. 'Problem, Pete?' one asked casually.

'No problem, mate,' I replied. 'This is the idiot who bottled me the other week.'

The mood of the three local guys changed in a split second when they realised that we were Marine Commandos and the pub was likely to be full of our mates. They apologised immediately and offered to buy the three of us as many pints as we wanted for the rest of the night. I think it also might have helped that Rob, who had asked whether I needed any help, was built like a brick shit-house and, incidentally, was the super-heavyweight boxing champion of the Marines!

But I think the Marines' survival training was probably more punishing than the beating I had suffered. For one week we had to survive in the open, living off the land with no shelter and, at the same time, avoiding probing enemy forces who were searching for us. It was explained to us that we were having to survive alone and behind enemy lines, cut off from friendly forces. We were provided with very little, simply a 4-ounce tobacco tin containing a small button compass, a rubber contraceptive, three small fish hooks and a line, a needle and thread, and fire-lighting strikers.

At midnight, we were taken to the drill shed and strip-searched, issued with a pair of overalls, an old jacket and a pair of socks and boots and taken in a 4-ton truck some 50 miles from base.

After being dropped, we were marched some 18 miles in pitch darkness and then permitted to get a couple of hours' sleep somewhere in the middle of a wood. For the first two days we were taught how to survive, learning how to catch wild rabbits, skin and cook them, as well as learning what vegetation we could eat and which we should avoid. The instructors showed us how to make clothes from anything we could find, how to make weapons for protection and hunting and how to navigate by the stars. We had brought no food with us and, as a consequence, by the end of the second day we were all but starving. By night we were taken on forced marches, having to navigate by the stars and sketch maps, and during the day we would have to try and find something to eat and have a few hours' sleep. Once, and only once, two of the lads who had sewn some money into their clothing popped into a shop somewhere on the moors we passed and bought some food. But they had been spotted. As punishment they were made to spend the following few hours running up and down a hill with large rocks in their arms until they were on the verge of passing out. They never repeated their misdemeanour and we never forgot their punishment. As I watched the poor bastards running up and down that hill, I had never dreamed that Marine Commandos could be so tough and so unrelenting. By the end of that week, we looked like refugees who had been living rough for months, surviving with very little food or sleep, looking dirty and scruffy and stinking of stale sweat and dirt. We looked pale and drawn and had obviously lost pounds in weight. And yet something inside me made me determined to succeed, to show that I could take everything they threw at me, and still survive.

Back at camp, we were told to shower and shave before tea, which smelt fantastic. We piled our plates high and sat down to gorge ourselves. Within three minutes none of us could eat any more — our stomachs had shrunk so much, we just sat and roared with laughter. That weekend we were free to go into town, drinking, dancing and making merry. In fact, we all spent the 48 hours in barracks — fast asleep in our beds!

But most of the Royal Marine Commando training appeared to consist of pushing us as hard as possible to attain peak physical fitness, so that by the end of the 30-week course those that lasted the distance were hardened, tough young men, capable of undertaking long, hard forced marches under the toughest conditions and carrying a full pack, a weapon and ammunition. But I have to admit that I felt it had all been well worth while when I was finally awarded the coveted Green Beret at the passing-out parade. That weekend — which also saw my nineteenth birthday — was wonderful, relaxing and boozy. But I was in for some surprises when I arrived at l Troop, Alpha Company of 40 Commando in Taunton to start my life as a fully-fledged professional of the Royal Marines.

* * *

Life as a Marine Commando was a tough, non-stop regime of constant physical training, military training, weapons training and more demanding, hard physical workouts. We remained supremely fit and healthy and alcohol didn't pass our lips for days at a time. Thursday night, however, was the troop's night on the town. I had never drunk so much, partied so hard or suffered such horrendous hangovers in my life. Nor shall I ever forget that first Thursday night as a member of the élite unit of Marine Commandos.

As I was dressing in a smart pair of jeans and

new shirt, I looked up to see other members of the troop coming into our barracks. One was dressed in a nurse's uniform, another as a female German officer, a third as a street Arab, and a fourth as a transvestite.

'What the fuck's going on?' I said, totally bewildered.

'Piss-up,' replied the nurse.

'Why the fancy dress?' I asked.

'More fun dressed like this,' replied the Arab.

'But you can't go dressed like that,' said the German officer who was wearing a blonde wig with long pig-tails under her cap. 'Someone will think you're an odd-ball if you dress in jeans and a shirt.'

'But that's the way I always dress for a night on the town,' I protested.

'Not any more you don't, lovey,' said the nurse camping it up, throwing me a mini-skirt, a girl's blouse, a wig and make-up. 'Here you are, these should fit you,' she added.

As 15 of us walked out of the camp, all dressed in the most outlandish gear, no one took the slightest notice, accepting our bizarre apparel as though we were in army uniform. I felt like a complete idiot and wanted to keep running back to the barracks to change. But after a short while I felt that this bizarre outfit could be a bit of fun and decided to enjoy myself. None of the barmaids or the pub landlord took the slightest notice of our appearance and happily served us, sometimes shaking their heads in disbelief, for they knew that we were all Marine Commandos, renowned as the toughest soldiers in the British special forces, with most of us dressed like girls on a night out. The drinking, the intake of such copious amounts of beer and chasers, was something else and I remember virtually nothing of that first night on the town. We only stopped drinking when we couldn't walk and the pub landlord happily called taxis to take us back to camp.

The following morning, I awoke with my head thumping, my mouth dry and still wearing my girls' outfit. Somehow I dragged myself out of bed, showered, and pulled on my PE kit. Everyone looked like death warmed up. As roll call was taken our attention was drawn to a figure running flat out into the camp and towards our ranks. It was 'Gladys', one of my mates who had decided to dress as a nurse and adopted the name Gladys, because his second name was Knight. He ran to the lines, fell in and was standing to attention still dressed in his nurse's uniform in torn black stockings, high heels and make-up. Our Sergeant couldn't resist a smile, told him to 'fuck off' and change into PE gear pronto and return in two minutes. He made it on time but had forgotten to take off his make-up. At first, the troop and particularly the NCOs tried to keep straight faces but it was impossible; and finally everyone just burst out laughing. Friday lunch was the start of our weekend and because I was only 30 minutes away on my Kawasaki 750cc, I spent most weekends at home with my mates, relaxing and resting, preparing for the next week's duties as a keen member of 40 Commando.

That first weekend back home I was having a beer with my pals Mike and Marcus when I was introduced to a girl by the name of Clare. We chatted, laughed and enjoyed each other's company and I thought she was lovely. It crossed my mind at the time that she may have fancied me because I certainly fancied her. But we didn't make a date and I didn't take her address or phone number and, although I thought of her often during the following weeks and months, we were not destined to see each other for four more years. But I never forgot the dark, bubbly teenager with the ready smile and searching eyes.

After several months of hard graft with 40 Commando, I discovered that I was constantly short of money and needed to find another job. Every month I was finding that I was skint more than a week before the next pay packet. So I decided to find a job to supplement my constant spending. So I went into showbusiness, volunteering to work as a 'Gorilla Gram'!

On the first night, there was no demand for a gorilla, but from then on I was constantly booked. Most of the time I was engaged to attend birthday parties or hen nights and would arrive on my Kawasaki dressed in my gorilla costume. I only needed to exchange my helmet for the gorilla's head and I was ready for action. I would usually prance around a bit in front of the party, making the appropriate gorilla noises before picking up the 'lucky' girl, throwing her over my shoulder and carrying her off down the road 100 yards or so. Everyone took it in good spirits and I did pubs, clubs, private houses, birthday parties, weddings and university graduation celebrations.

Only once did I have any real bother and that was when I was physically attacked by a group of about ten women who were determined to strip me of my gorilla outfit and God knows what they intended to do with me. Initially, I saw their attention as a joke, but when I was lying on the floor with crazed women tearing at my gorilla outfit, screaming 'Get 'em off, get 'em off,' I feared the worst and knew that if I didn't make an escape the gorilla suit would be trashed and I would probably end up stark bollock naked. I thought it would be easy to shake them off and leave, but they proved very persistent and remarkably strong. Eventually, I managed to escape, ran outside and leapt on my bike as the gaggle of women raced after me shouting obscenities and demands to strip me naked. But after a few weeks, I realised the money I was earning didn't compensate for the social life I was missing with my mates, so I decided to pack in the job. The boss offered me promotion — working as Tarzan — but I declined. It was the end of my career in entertainment!

Life in the Marines could also have its moments, and I have to admit I've had my fair share of scrapes. Gladys and I were on exercises on the troop carrier HMS Intrepid and had dropped anchor off Gibraltar. We had been given shore leave and, understandably, had enjoyed a great night out touring the bars and the nightclubs. But we missed the last boat back to Intrepid and knew we would be in severe trouble if we didn't make it back to the ship before daybreak. Suddenly, in our drunken state, we had what we believed to be a brilliant idea. We would borrow a boat from the marina and, if necessary, row over to HMS Intrepid. We found a small rowing boat with an outboard motor and took that, edging out into the harbour with me at the oars and Gladys struggling to start the outboard. We were going quite well when suddenly we went from pitch dark to broad daylight, or so it seemed. Fast motor torpedo boats were racing towards us, searchlights picking us out, and Military Police and local police officers were shouting from the harbour to stop rowing and put our hands above our heads. As the speed boats appproached us we heard weapons being cocked and in that split second I wondered if someone was actually going to open fire. Then I heard a distant voice I recognised, one of our Colour-Sergeants yelling at us, 'What the fuck are you two playing at?'

At that moment I realised we were for the high jump, but I felt relieved that we weren't about to be shot. We turned and made our way back to the harbour which was covered in Military Police and Gibraltar cops with their car, jeep and truck headlights on and the blue lights flashing as though in a movie. Only this was for real and we were in the shit.

'I've managed to calm both the Gibraltar Police and the MPs but I've told both of them that you will be severely dealt with back on board ship. You could have been smugglers or political activists or even fucking terrorists trying to put a mine on the ship,' he explained in a loud voice, making us feel absolute idiots. Back on board, the Colour-Sergeant gave us a right bollocking and then told us to go below and forget about it. We were lucky.

But I didn't always enjoy such luck. In fact, during that overseas trip, I was fortunate not to die but it had nothing to do with guns or weapons or misbehaving. We were in the middle of a desert, 100 miles or so from Alexandria on military exercises with units of the Egyptian Army. We had enjoyed the few days as tourists in the dust and mayhem of crowded Alexandria, visiting bazaars and street markets, fighting off the beggars, traders and the kids pestering us for money. I was eventually persuaded to buy a brass plate to take back home as a present for my parents.

But our time in the desert, including large-scale exercises involving rocket launchers, heavy guns and tanks, would be very useful training for later in my military career. The heat, of course, was oppressive, the forced marches in the sand absolute hell, but the weather, with the temperature somewhere in the nineties, did give us all great suntans which made up for some of the discomfort and hard graft. One morning, however, I awoke feeling bloody awful and trudged off to the sick bay. Within 12 hours I was suffering from a severe fever, high temperature, stomach cramps and appalling diarrhoea. As I returned after one of my many visits to the latrines that night, I stooped to get into the tent and collapsed in a heap. The next thing I remember was waking up in the sick bay with two intravenous drips in my arms, my body packed in ice and the doctors making plans to airlift me to hospital. I heard someone describe my condition as 'critical', so I gathered I must have been pretty ill. But I kept drifting into unconsciousness and came to my senses to find myself in a modern, well-equipped hospital ward being tended to by smart, efficient Egyptian nurses. I and a few others, who had also been struck down by what we believed was the result of eating some dodgy chicken, were kept in hospital under observation for nearly a week before being permitted to leave and rejoin our units.

Twenty-four hours later, we were informed that we were to carry out an 'advance to contact' exercise with Egyptian Commandos using live ammunition. That sent many of the old sweats into something of a hot flush for they had experienced such exercises involving third-world armies in the past and had been lucky to live to tell the tale.

'For God's sake, keep your fucking heads down,' we were told, 'and take no risks because you never know what the fuck might happen. Keep your wits about you.'

We were told that both the Egyptian and the British forces would only be firing sporadically throughout the exercise to conserve ammunition and for safety's sake. We had, of course, taken part in live ammo exercises on many occasions and we knew the drill. But I hoped the Egyptians knew the drill, too. Unfortunately, they hadn't the slightest idea how to carry out such an exercise. The start went fine. Everybody seemed to know exactly what to do until the moment the fire control order was given.

As instructed, we began putting down effective suppressing fire when suddenly the Egyptian Commandos opened up. It sounded like every Rambo film ever produced suddenly played together in the space of a few minutes. The noise was deafening and it was obvious the Egyptians had simply put their weapons on automatic and gone wild. We looked at each other in disbelief. And then, as suddenly as the chaos had started, there was silence. In the space of five minutes, they had used up every round they had, including their spare ammo. As instructed, we were still on our first magazines. But despite some heartfelt concern amongst the officers in command that we were running a serious risk of being accidentally shot, it was decided to continue with the exercise. Somehow, no one was actually injured. But it had been a narrow escape.

CHAPTER THREE

From the moment I first put on that green beret, I sensed that I was a member of an élite unit, privileged to be accepted into such a band of dedicated, highly professional soldiers. It appeared to me that they aspired to the highest ideals of military expertise, believing their regiment — the Royal Marine Commandos — to be one of the best in the world.

The Special Boat Service was the brain-child of an East African big-game hunter, Roger Courtney, who had spent much of the 1930s paddling his canoe from Lake Victoria down the Nile and into Egypt. Courtney was a big man in every sense of the word, with a bellow of a laugh, who could drink the equivalent of two men under a Mess table. He came to England at the outbreak of World War II, determined to persuade the powers that be that the Royal Navy should consider using flimsy, wooden-framed, canvas-topped canoes. The idea was instantly dismissed as ridiculous and foolhardy even by the daring, adventurous staff of Combined Services. But Roger Courtney would not take 'no' for an answer.

During a conference of senior officers of Combined Operations held at a hotel on the banks of the Clyde in Scotland in June 1940, Courtney set out to prove that his idea was not only sound but could also be highly practical and expedient. While the officers were in the middle of discussions about the organisation and control of commando units, Courtney walked uninvited into the hotel, barged his way into the conference room and plonked a canvas gun cover from HMS Glengyle on to the table. The Glengyle was, at the time, lying at anchor in the bay.

'What the hell is this?' one officer spluttered indignantly. 'Who are you? Who the hell let you in here?'

Two officers got to their feet and were about to escort Courtney from the room when the giant of a man raised his hand and told the officers he had come in peace. He explained that he had no intention of causing trouble, but was only trying to persuade those present that his idea of using canoes was not as daft as they had imagined. Fortunately, one officer attending the meeting recognised Courtney as the big-game hunter who had been trying to sell the Royal Navy the crackpot idea of using canvas-topped canoes as a weapon of war.

'Earlier this evening, gentlemen,' he explained with some aplomb, 'I and another canoeist paddled one of our canoes out into the bay to the Glengyle. I climbed up the anchor chain and removed this gun cover which you see on the table. No one saw us and no one tried to stop us because those on duty had no idea that we were there. To them, we were invisible. I have only carried out this experiment to show you how useful canoes could be in some types of naval operations requiring secrecy and stealth.'

'You could easily have got yourself killed, you know,' said one senior officer. Courtney explained that he had fully realised the risk he had taken approaching a Royal Naval vessel in a canoe, but that he had taken the risk because he was almost certain that no one on board would have been aware of his presence. 'I have so much confidence in the expediency of these canoes to take enemy ships at anchor by surprise, that I was certain we would not be noticed. As you can see, gentlemen, it worked.'

Courtney's ruse worked, but the officers present were not wholly convinced. After discussing the matter in more detail, the officers issued Courtney with another challenge to prove that his idea could be both practical and successful. They challenged him to paddle his canoe once again to the Glengyle, and leave chalk marks on the hull where he would have planted limpet-mines. Happily, Courtney accepted the challenge. The following night, he paddled out to the Glengyle again and reached the ship without being sighted. Carefully, he drew the chalk marks on the hull and, seeing an open port-hole, he decided to gain access in the hope of stealing something and returning triumphantly a second time to the sceptical officers waiting on shore. But, unknown to Courtney, the ship's crew had been alerted and, as he climbed through the port-hole, he was caught red-handed. It didn't matter, however, for the following morning he was able to show the officers the chalk marks he had made.

Those demonstrations heralded the beginning of the Special Boat Service. As a direct result of his daring and cheek, Courtney was given permission to train canoe sections with the idea of eventually attaching one such 30-man section to each commando unit.

Courtney had used a simple sporting canoe manufactured by the Folbot Company, which had gone out of business in 1940, but because of Courtney's exploits the name lived on for decades. Officially, though, the canoes were called 'Cockles' and the naval personnel who manned them would become a legend, known as 'Cockleshell Heroes'.

The first successful wartime operation against the enemy took place in February 1941 off the coast of the Greek island of Rhodes, after General Wavell had given the order to seize the island. On five occasions prior to the invasion, Courtney took the helm of a canoe in the dead of night while a Royal Navy officer sat up front. When the canoe was close enough to the coastline, the officer slipped silently overboard to swim ashore and check out the shoreline for enemy fortifications or gun emplacements. The operations were totally successful and the SBS had proved itself to be a new and competent part of commando operations.

The first demolition raid behind enemy lines was carried out by Courtney's second-in-command, Lieutenant 'Tug' Wilson, Royal Artillery, a canoe fanatic, and Marine Hughes who had joined the Royal Marines in 1939. Their names would become legendary in the wartime history of the SBS. In this first ever SBS raid, the two men blew up an ammunition train on the coast of Sicily, having planted explosives under the line. Both men returned safely to their mother ship. It was the forerunner of many such daring and highly dangerous operations against enemy installations throughout the Mediterranean, which caused consternation among the enemy ranks and gave the Allies another valuable fighting arm. At that time, it was decided to place the SBS under the command of Colonel David Stirling, the founder of the Special Air Service, the legendary SAS.

So successful was the small band of daring canoeists, that senior naval officers became quickly convinced that the use of canoes should be considered in all operations carried out close to enemy shorelines. After the early successes in the Mediterranean, members of the SBS carried out valuable demolition strikes against German defences in Norway and Sweden, but the main historical stream of SBS sabotage raiding rested with the squadrons based in the Mediterranean between 1942 and 1945. Throughout World War II, of course, the SBS also played a vital part in placing and evacuating secret agents behind enemy lines, particularly across the entire Mediterranean theatre and later in the Far East.

But the bloodiest series of raids in SBS history took place between November 1943 and the spring of the following year, all directed by Headquarters Raiding Forces Middle East from Cairo under the command of Lieutenant-Colonel Turnbull. The first raid on the German-held island of Simi off the Turkish coast in November 1943 was a copy-book SBS operation. A small force of German infantry, comprising 18 German soldiers, 60 Italians, and a small police force and ten 'cooks and bottle washers' held the island, but they were no match for the two SBS patrols which went ashore. Under the light of a full moon, one patrol moved into the town of Kastello, moving quietly over the rubble of buildings decimated in earlier bombing raids. As they were quietly making their way into the Governor's castle, they disturbed a German machine-gun nest. One SBS officer threw a grenade at the detachment and after the machine-gun ceased firing they could hear the groans of wounded men. An SBS Sergeant grabbed a German Schmeisser from the wounded men as seven German soldiers ran along the pier towards him, firing all the time. The Sergeant stood his ground and at around 30 metres opened fire on the charging troops, killing all seven. Other SBS men laid a 10kg explosive under the castle, razing it to the ground. Its job completed, the patrol retreated as more Germans and Italians raced towards the castle in a bid to wipe out the enemy raiders. But a booby-trap charge had been placed in the street causing their pursuers to activate it, resulting in more dead and wounded.

But the heroic deeds of the SBS patrol were not yet over. They torched the local boat yard, attacked the island's power station, putting it out of action, and then killed eight more enemy soldiers in a fierce ten-minute fire-fight. The SBS two-man Bren-gun team replied to fire from the harbour guard, but it is not known if any were killed or wounded. By the time the SBS patrol had withdrawn, nearly all the garrison had been killed or wounded and not a single SBS man had been lost. It was a classic SBS raid, short, sharp and devastating, which had taken the defenders by surprise. It also set the pattern for subsequent raids.

So fearful had Hitler become that the Allies would attack Germany through Greece, that he sent Rommel to inspect German defences in the Balkans and set up an outer ring of eleven garrisoned islands in the Aegean, reinforced by the crack German brigade from XXI Mountain Corps and the infantry of 999 Division. The islands proved a magnificent proving ground for the SBS. And, as a result of a number of dramatically successful raids against German and Italian troops manning these outposts, General von Klemann, who had been put in command of the defensive ring of islands, decided to abandon many of the smaller sites. He introduced a policy of putting large garrisons on single islands for several weeks at a time and then moving on to another island. It was as a result of these rapid, ruthless and successful attacks against much larger forces that the SBS earned the title 'The Invisible Raiders'. From October 1943 to the spring of 1945, the SBS carried out a total of 381 raids on around 70 islands in the Aegean.

Occasionally, of course, plans went awry. But when that occurred, the heroism of SBS troops was truly remarkable. One of the stories told and re-told to successive SBS recruits proved the necessity of the regiment's back-breaking training schedules which became a legend even among Special Forces.

It began with a daring SBS night raid on German-held Tobruk in North Africa in August 1942, in a bid to knock out German shore installations and communications and, hopefully, to hinder their advance into Egypt. The SBS squad had been brought in to guide detachments of Royal Engineers and the Special Air Service into Tobruk to coincide with the night-time landing of the 11th Battalion Royal Marines, 150 infantry men and two sections of machine-gunners.

First, the SBS men were taken by surprise when a German machine-gun detachment opened fire shortly after they had landed, scattering the advance party and putting the entire mission in danger of postponement. That machine-gun nest was destroyed by a single SBS officer. While his mates kept the German machine-gunners busy, the SBS officer courageously ran directly at the emplacement and shot dead the four-man German squad with his submachine-gun.

As the SBS team ran along the beach towards the spot where the Infantry were expected to land, they came across a German wireless station set up in a building near the beach. They approached behind cover and then dashed towards the building, taking the guards by surprise and killing them all before racing inside and raking the ops room with their submachine-guns, killing the remaining operators and staff, most of whom had been killed when grenades had been lobbed into the staff quarters. They then set charges and detonated them, blowing up the entire building.

Back on the beach, the SBS squad were facing serious trouble. Nothing was going according to plan. Lieutenant Tommy Langton of the SBS went alone on to the beach to guide the incoming MTBs (motor torpedo boats) by flash light. From aerial photographs, the SBS and the Commandos knew there were numbers of German troops defending that part of the shoreline but they weren't sure precisely how many.

Langton could see that the landing craft were in serious difficulties and apparently unable to make the beach. Several MTBs appeared to have stopped dead in the water, while others looked as though they were having problems with steering. It seemed to Langton that his small SBS troop was in danger of being cut off, which would entail having to battle their way to the beach in a fighting retreat without the help of the more heavily armed Marine Commandos. As Lieutenant Langton was making wireless contact with the ships lying offshore in the darkness, the beach was suddenly illuminated by searchlights and, within a matter of seconds, the Germans, securely dug-in, opened fire. Chaos ensued. The Germans began shelling the MTBs causing serious damage, and more than half the force were destroyed. Most of the troops who did manage to make it to the beach were killed, wounded or taken prisoner. In the aftermath of the attack, HMS Sikh was sunk by heavy shore batteries, called into action when the MTBs were sighted, and HMS Coventry and the destroyer HMS Zulu were sunk by German Stuka dive-bombers.

However, Tommy Langton and two private soldiers who had been together on the beach somehow survived and rounded up 25 soldiers who had managed to struggle ashore only to find themselves pinned down under heavy machine-gun fire. Refusing to surrender to the enemy, Langton led the group on what seemed an impossible march, an extraordinary journey to safety — a 700-mile trek through the scorching desert with little food or water. At times during their trek, they were strafed by patrolling Luftwaffe fighters. Their journey was to last 78 days and for the final three weeks they trudged through the burning sand in bare feet! Day by day, the group became smaller, victims of dysentery, starvation, exhaustion, capture and the occasional brush with marauding German patrols. After three weeks, the group was down to six men; then three. Finally, Tommy Langton and the two privates, exhausted, starving, bedraggled and near to death, reached the Allied lines. It was a supreme example of determination and physical fitness which would enter the annals of SBS history, never to be forgotten.

While some SBS raiders caused problems for the German land forces in North Africa and the Aegean, other SBS commandos were taking part in raiding parties against the German forces occupying the French Channel coast. From 1942 onwards, SBS patrols were involved in innumerable missions, collecting military intelligence, making recce raids almost at will and frequently causing confusion and consternation among the German defenders, as they would suddenly strike against entrenched German forces with speed and surprise. More importantly, these raids caused significant headaches for the German High Command.

It was known that the British, probably supported by the Americans, would one day launch an invasion of Europe, but the question always remained — where exactly would the Allies forces strike? Constantly, SBS raiding parties would mount surprise attacks on German defences at different places along the coast, deliberately confusing the senior German commanders. Sometimes, the SBS and SAS troops would parachute into France behind enemy lines; at other times MTBs would drop them off and they would swim ashore, climb the cliffs and then abseil back down again when their mission was accomplished. On other occasions, they would silently paddle their canoes on to the beach immediately beneath German fortifications to make accurate recces or to raid some German fortification, kill a few guards, and then make good their escape before the German defenders realised what was happening. But, without fail, every action the SBS troops undertook on those raids into occupied France was highly dangerous, needing courage, stamina, discipline and sometimes a little luck.

But those SBS forces who had spent most of the war successfully attacking islands in the Aegean and Mediterranean found their experience extremely valuable when they came to raiding even stronger German defences around the Adriatic. SBS recce teams found well-defended garrisons on the islands in the Gulf of Fiume where the German strongholds were more extensive and sophisticated, employing anti-personnel minefields, wire entanglements, dogs and alert sentries.

One of the SBS's most dangerous exploits was an attack on the Villa Punta, a fortified house overlooking a beach on the island of Losinj in the Adriatic, which was defended by a garrison of 45 Germans, who had reinforced the cellars of the rambling old mansion. In February 1945, an SBS unit of 17 men, under the command of Captain

Ambrose McGonigal, was ordered to clear the building. He planned to draw the German defenders to the rear of the house and then break in through the front door. But it didn't quite work out like that. When one group of four SBS men were making their way along the beach, they ran into barbed wire, alerting a guard who opened fire. He was joined by a fighting patrol who moved out to attack the four SBS soldiers. But supporting SBS Bren-gunners on the garden walls drove the attacking Germans back into the house. McGonigal then lead his team into the building, breaking down the front door while Bren-gunners kept the Germans pinned towards the rear of the building. In a classic operation, the SBS men, working in pairs, began clearing the house, passage by passage, room by room, which proved an almost impossible task in the darkness, illuminated only by exploding grenades and flares. The SBS Bren-gunners outside the house could not, of course, tell friend from foe, and, as a result, the SBS troops had very little support from covering fire.

As James Ladd explained in The History of the Special Boat Service, 'The dark of the passages was lit by the occasional flash of a grenade, while the sudden noise of firing — the ripping of a Schmeisser's rapid fire, answered by the slower staccato of Sten or Tommy gun — seemed to reverberate in all directions. The shudder of explosions and the acrid smell of smoke added to the confusion, after spells of deathly silence broken only by occasional bursts of Bren fire raking the wooden shutters.'

Captain Jimmy Lees was shot dead after he failed to clear a room of Germans; Marine Kitchingham was shot dead when he threw open the door of what he believed was an empty room; and Lieutenant Jones-Parry, his left arm shattered and with a bullet lodged in his spleen, managed to re-load his submachine-gun with one hand and fire a burst of automatic killing the German gunner who had shot him. And still the SBS team continued to clear the rooms until the entire place was a mass of flames. With only 11 men still fit and carrying others seriously wounded in the fire-fight, McGonigal made a fighting withdrawal to the motor-launch two miles distant. Somehow, the SBS men made it back to base but serious lessons had been learnt — dislodging determined men from secure defensive positions had become that much more difficult.

Two months later, another SBS unit, again commanded by Captain McGonigal, was ordered to break a German defence position, guarded by 80 men, who were holding a bridge on the vital junction linking the islands of Cres and Losinj in the Gulf of Fiume. After a seven-mile trek along a concealed approach to Osor, the village by the bridge, the SBS unit of 30 men were spotted before they could take out the strongholds surrounding the main German defences. The high walls around the gardens of the group of houses occupied by the Germans had been protected by barbed wire, but the SBS knew a way had to be found through the German defences if the bridge was to be taken. Lieutenant Henshaw volunteered to take the most extraordinary gamble and try to cross open ground to cut a hole through the wire. But as he reached the wire and began cutting, he was spotted and a hail of grenades were hurled at him, killing him. With eight German machine-guns covering every defensive angle, it was impossible for the SBS teams to make any headway. They did, however, force their way forward whenever an opportunity arose and managed to kill or wound half the German forces before their ammunition ran dangerously low. McGonigal decided to retreat but he was annoyed that he had been unable to dislodge the defenders.

Throughout World War II, the Special Boat Squadron had their fair share of heroes, but none more so than a young Dane, Anders Lassen, a former cadet in the Danish Merchant Navy, who joined the British Army in 1940, and was later commissioned into the SBS. He had been involved in many daring SBS raids, always showing extraordinary valour and taking greater risks than those men who served with him.

Major Lassen, aged 25, took command of a 60-strong SBS assault group which also included 50 men of 42 Field Company of the Royal Engineers, and 60 Italian Resistance fighters in 'Operation Fry'. This daring mission was designed to persuade German Field Marshal Kesselring that the Allies were about to launch their major invasion through Comacchio on the River Po in northern Italy.

Anders Lassen and his assault squad were ordered to take four islands above the flood waters south-west of the heavily defended town of Comacchio. The four groups set off in punts across the muddy waters of Lake Comacchio and managed to take islands number 3 and 4 quite easily, but the other two islands were more heavily fortified. Then the SBS took to their collapsible canoes for the final push and caught the defenders of island number 2 by surprise in a brief and bloody assault. There remained only the prize of striking at the heart of Comacchio itself and, after paddling their canoes across the still waters of the lake, Lassen decided to lead the assault on the town. The courageous five SBS men had advanced nearly half a mile in the dead of night along the dyke road when they were challenged. One SBS who could speak fluent Italian replied that they were fishermen returning home, but when asked to step into the centre of the road the Germans opened fire. The other four dived for cover and Lassen decided he had to take out what he perceived to be a German pillbox, manned by machine-gunners, 400 yards along the road. He ordered the others to stay behind and worked his way in the lee of the dyke to the roadside opposite the strongpoint. He then hurled two grenades into the centre of the machine-gun nest, killing the four Germans.

Further along the road were two more machine-gun posts, which Lassen knew had to be taken if the mission was to succeed and so he decided to repeat the process despite the fact that the German machine-gunners, now fearful that they were facing a determined and serious assault, were firing away at will. In the ensuing fire-fight one SBS man was killed by a direct hit, another was seriously wounded. While the other two men dragged their wounded colleague to safety, Lassen went on alone to tackle the two enemy machine-gun posts.

Lassen made his way to within 50 yards of the next German machine-gun nest and when someone shouted 'Kamerad', Lassen decided to risk all and stood up pretending that he was a German soldier. They were not fooled and Lassen was blasted by rapid machine-gun fire from almost point-blank range. Mortally wounded, Lassen managed somehow to crawl back to the others.

'Get the wounded back to safety,' he said, hardly able to talk, 'I'll stay here and hold them off.'

'We won't leave you,' said one of the SBS men.

'This is an order,' said Lassen, 'save the others. I'm finished.'

They were his last words. As the others left, taking their wounded colleague with them, Lassen summoned up enough strength to throw three more grenades to cover his men's withdrawal. Lassen's body was found on the road where he had died, aged 25. For his courage and leadership, Lassen was awarded a posthumous VC.

The single, most spectacular raid that would catapult the Special Boat Squadron to legendary status, as well as creating national heroes, began at 2000 hours on Monday, December 7 1942, when five 'Cockle' canoes were launched from the submarine, HMS Tuna. The Cockles were a new, stronger type of canoe which were designed to be launched into action from submarines. A canoe, with two paddlers, was hoisted from the submarine casing by tackle fitted to a girder extension from the muzzle of the submarine's 4-inch gun. The gun was then swung round to lower the canoe into the water. The concept behind the new Cockles was to enable them to attack enemy ships as they lay in harbour or at anchor.

The first raid, however, was a straightforward, conventional anti-shipping attack against German vessels laid up in Bordeaux, an attack which, using conventional assault landing forces, would have involved 20,000 men and massive air raids. This new-style SBS attack required only 12 men. The canoeists were to paddle by night and lay up by day and though the 70 miles of the Gironde river banks were patrolled by German forces, the sea would be the most hazardous part of their epic journey. Two canoes were lost as they made their way from the Bay of Biscay to the river and five days later only two of the canoes reached their destination, planting limpet mines on five German ships laid at anchor. Four ships were badly damaged but, more than that, the mission proved the extraordinary capabilities of the SBS. Unfortunately, the fate of those Cockleshell Heroes who had been captured during the operation was severe. Seven were summarily shot without trial by the Germans, one escaped through Spain and their leader, Major 'Blondie' Hasler and Marine Bill Sparks successfully came out on the French Resistance 'Pat' escape line. Despite the seven summary executions, the official history of Combined Operations described the result 'of this brilliant little operation' as a good example of the 'successful use of limpeteers'.

As the war in Europe developed into the more traditional air and land battles, the SBS and other members of Combined Operations concentrated more on Japan and the Far East where there was enormous scope for SBS-type activities with the thousands of islands and millions of miles of vulnerable coastline. When

Admiral Lord Louis Mountbatten took over as Supreme Commander in southeast Asia in 1943 he set up SOG — the Small Operations Group — to encompass such units as the SBS and COPPs (Combined Operations Pilotage Parties). In essence, members of COPPs were swimmer-canoeists, men capable of taking care of themselves in all circumstances who had navigational training. Such men would be delivered by submarine, landing craft and other means, paddle inshore in their canoes, and then slip over the side to recce a shoreline and draft maps and charts to ensure the safe landing of Allied troops.

As a consequence, COPPs were informed of top-secret Allied invasion plans months ahead of their launch and permission for this was given by Prime Minister Winston Churchill himself. In fact, COPPs only worked under cover of the Official Secrets Act; their existence was never referred to in any newspaper, BBC broadcasts or even internal services memos. Their knowledge of future secret Allied battle plans did, however, put them in an impossible position if captured and, to make matters worse, many of their exploits entailed working in enemy territory and often behind enemy lines. Indeed, three COPP officers were understood to have swum out to sea and drowned rather than face torture by Japanese forces waiting on shore. All COPP volunteers were always provided with cyanide pills before every mission.

Mountbatten believed that accurate recces were a vital part of successful assaults on beaches and, in most cases, these were carried out by COPPs who would provide detailed descriptions of beaches and their defences for Allied landings. At the moment of invasion, COPPs would wait aboard their canoes, anchored 100 yards off the beach, shining shaded torches out to sea to guide in the assault ships and landing craft. In one landing alone, four canoes guided in 3,250 ships. In essence, the COPP would be the pioneer of modern beach recces.

Even during World War II, selection and training for both the SBS and COPPs was rigorous. Only 10 per cent of those who applied were selected for training and only 10 per cent of those actually passed the tough four-month course. The power handed to COPPs volunteers, many of whom were SBS personnel, was unprecedented. With Churchill's full backing,

Mountbatten was granted permission by the Chiefs of Staff to give absolute priority in all circumstances to the COPP teams. As a result, Mountbatten then gave formal orders to all COPP officers that if any of them ever experienced any difficulty whatsoever from any senior officer of whatever rank, then the officer should immediately get in touch by phone with the Chief of Combined Operations — Mountbatten himself. Even a lowly corporal in charge of a COPP outfit had this extraordinary authority. The senior officers of all three services did not like the orders but they obeyed them to the letter.

Indeed, COPPs became a vital and integral part of all Allied invasions in every war theatre. They took part in the Sicily landings and, of course, in the greatest invasion of history, the Normandy landings, as well as operations throughout South-East Asia. In the last two months of World War II, COPPs and the SBS mounted 174 raiding and recce operations behind Japanese lines, carrying out vital missions with little or no regard for their own safety.

* * *

Throughout its history, the selection process for

those volunteering for the Special Boat Squadron has always been unrelenting and rigorous. Recruits had to be men with sufficient physical and mental stamina to sustain them through the most difficult times. They were mainly loners and survivors, individualists with great strength of character. Their motivation was undemonstrative patriotism, youthful adventure, self-reliance, independence of mind; often quiet fellows but full of spirit.

After World War II, however, when many special units were disbanded, the SBS was kept on under the wing of the Royal Marines and their valuable expertise was called on in various wars, including Borneo and Brunei, as well as the Communist insurgency in Malaya and, of course, in Korea. It was during the Korean War that many of the stratagems and devices first put into practice during World War II were extensively used, and to great effect. SBS forces, sometimes working with the American Underwater Demolition Team, were involved in daring raids into North Korean territory.

From the start of the war, both Russian and Chinese military hardware was being transported almost daily into North Korea in a massive effort to bolster the Communist North Korea Government which had invaded the non-Communist south of the country. It was vital to the United Nations forces that the railway link running from Russia and China down the eastern side of North Korea, and along which the great majority of the arms and supplies were moved, should be attacked and destroyed. This mission was an ideal operation for the SBS, backed by the Americans, to prove their capabilities and their military prowess. As a result, one of the first such raids occurred in October 1950 when the USS Perch dropped four SBS officers and 63 other ranks into inflatables which were then towed into the shore by a motor boat which the Perch carried in a cylindrical hangar abaft the conning tower. The motor boat was launched five miles from the shore and then towed the raiding craft to within 400 yards of the beach. American swimmers then carried out a shore recce and subsequently signalled in the SBS raiders, who took with them anti-tank mines to set beneath the railway lines. As the raiders were making their way back to the Perch, they heard the mines exploding. A few nights later, further down the track SBS raiders, using the same covert approach, towed ashore

2,000 kilograms of explosives which they laid under culverts, bridges and in the walls of a railway tunnel along the same stretch of railway. Once again, as the SBS Marines made good their escape, they heard the satisfying blasts of the massive explosions — it took the North Koreans weeks to repair the damage.

The SBS were later given permission to conduct as many raids as they wished on the north-east Korean coast, so they set up a forward base of operations on Yo Do Island, the small mile-long island 100 miles north of the main battlefront. SBS troops would remain in the forward base for two weeks at a time, taking with them mortars, tents, landing craft, canoes and rations for fourteen days. Then they would be replaced by another troop and take a well-deserved rest and recuperation on one of the other islands held by the South Koreans. These SBS Marines would recce coastal battery positions at close range, passing on the details to US destroyers who would shell the batteries. Other SBS Marines would land on tiny islands for days at a time and report shipping and troop movements by radio. Two years later, all the SBS personnel were withdrawn from the Korean War having won 15 awards for gallantry.

But little was known at the time of the constant training and military exercises being undertaken by the SBS troops who were secretly patrolling the Rhine. NATO had decided that if the Russians decided to invade Western Europe, then the British Army of the Rhine would fall back to the first line of natural defence, the west bank of the river. The SBS role in any future conflict would be to use the Rhine as their hunting ground, disrupting and attacking Russian troop movements from the east. The SBS had been trained to provide recce and intelligence reports on troop concentrations and carry out sabotage raids, blow up the river barges and tugs, and create hazards to crossings; attack bridges and pontoons and destroy and sink Russian ships, making navigation of the Rhine extremely difficult. Full-scale exercises and training programmes were almost continuous and with the army manoeuvres and exercises at Brigade and Corps strength, the Russians were left in no doubt that the BAOR was serious.

In fact, secret SBS training went much further and during the early 1950s SBS marines were engaged in day-to-day tracking of Russian forces on the eastern side of the Rhine, shadowing Russian army movements and reporting back to BAOR headquarters by wireless. Throughout that period of intense Cold War activity, the SBS Marines were, in fact, involved in a series of covert operations over many years because they moved among Russian and East German forces on the eastern side of the Rhine, nearly always dressed in civilian-looking clothing. Some SBS men were, in fact, captured by the Russian forces and interrogated for hours, sometimes days, before being released and transported back to BAOR headquarters. The Russians liked to make a show of such occasions, thus demonstrating their ability to trap and capture what they termed 'British spies'.

That was why the Russians were only too happy to make a fuss about the disappearance of a British frogman, Commander 'Buster' Crabb, a Royal Navy diver and bomb disposal expert who, during World War II, had carried out innumerable feats of extraordinary courage in disarming enemy bombs under water with no fear for his own safety. One day in April 1956, Crabb, then 46 years old, was approached by an MI6 agent and asked if he would be prepared to examine the hull of a Russian cruiser, the Ordzhonikidze, when she arrived in Portsmouth with an escort of two battleships. The cruiser was carrying the two Soviet leaders, Kruschev and Bulganin, on a goodwill visit to Britain. 'Buster' Crabb readily agreed.

His task was to measure the cruiser's propeller and to discover how the ship managed to travel at twice the speed originally estimated by British naval intelligence. Commander Crabb booked into a Portsmouth hotel and shortly after the Ordzhonikidze had docked, Crabb, equipped with underwater breathing apparatus, entered the waters of Portsmouth harbour. He was never seen again. Much speculation followed and Prime Minister Anthony Eden faced mounting Commons criticism from opposition MPs demanding to know what Commander Crabb was doing in Portsmouth harbour, who had issued the instructions and what had become of the gallant Commander who had been considered a brave war hero. But Prime Minister Eden refused to reveal the truth, hiding behind the hoary old defence of 'national interest'.

The 'Buster' Crabb fiasco was not at all beneficial to the Special Boat Squadron; in fact, it was bloody awful public relations. From that moment, the SBS was under a cloud and quite wrongly so, but there was nothing that could be done about it. There was, of course, a problem. For the most part, the operations carried out by the SBS were deliberately kept under wraps in the same way as missions undertaken by the Special Air Service were kept quiet until the late 1980s when the national newspapers and book publishers came to realise that the public perceived the SAS as modern-day heroes, courageous dare-devils whom the reading public admired and adored. Those three letters — SAS — became a magnet to people searching for real-life adventure, something challenging and different, something to read and dream about as they went about their mundane lives. Fortunately for the Special Boat Squadron, however, the public had not yet 'discovered' the SBS; middle England had not yet come to realise that the SBS were in fact the crème de la crème of Special Forces and were renowned so throughout the military world.

By chance, a war far away in the desert kingdom of Oman in the Persian Gulf came to the rescue, and SBS personnel were drafted into this new trouble area to do their stuff. Once again, they carried out their missions with professionalism, earning the praise of the ruler, a recluse by the name of Sultan Said bin Talmur. But little or nothing was known of this secret war by the British general public. On the ground, however, the men of the Special Boat Squadron had to adapt almost overnight to the demands of their new environment, fighting a war in the desert rather than at sea. The kingdom of Muscat and Oman, as it was officially entitled, was in 1957 still a feudal administration with the Sultan having total command of the armed forces, the legislature and the judiciary, as he had done when he first came to power back in 1932!

Britain had been an ally of the Sultanate since 1798, but the alliance became infinitely more significant in the 1950s because Oman controlled the Musandam Peninsula which commanded the Hormuz Straits through which 50 per cent of the western world's oil supply passed. As a result of Arab nationalism that was gaining strength in the 1950s, various revolts, encouraged by outside forces, erupted in Oman and Muscat and the Sultan turned to Britain for military assistance to help put them down. Understandably, with the probability that Oman itself would discover valuable oil reserves, Britain was only too ready to help. The SBS were called in to undertake deep penetration patrols for which their training made them ideal. Patrols of 60 SBS swimmer-canoeists would be despatched to the more rugged desert areas, dominated by the rebels, where they would survive for long periods in the hellish heat of the day, which in the summer months tipped over 100° Fahrenheit. They survived only by conserving energy and water and living on animals they could track and kill.

One of the first major battles took place on the Jebel Akhdar, an arid, high, mountainous plateau where rebels had taken up commanding positions. The Sultan wanted the well-armed rebels dislodged and the SAS, backed by troops from the Royal Marines and the SBS, were thrown into the assault on the rebels' positions. The mini-war lasted for 30 days for the rebels commanded the heights and were well dug-in with supplies of modern military equipment and ample reserves of ammunition. Finally, the British forces gained control and routed the remaining gunmen who fled into Saudi Arabia.

What is not known, however, is that during that period the rebels were being supplied by the

Americans, and were ferried in buses owned by US oil companies who had discovered vast oil supplies in the Saudi Arabian deserts. The American oil companies were understandably keen to add Oman and Muscat to their area of influence, even though that meant encouraging rebel tribesman to take up arms against British forces engaged in helping an old ally remain in command of his kingdom. Understandably, the British Government was extremely angry with the US administration and demanded that the American oil companies be ordered to stop assisting the rebels. The matter, however, never came to the attention of the House of Commons and after receiving assurances from the US Government that the practice would cease, the British Government dropped their complaint. The whole matter — an astonishing action perpetrated by oil companies from such a close ally as the United States — was quietly forgotten.

Mini-wars and various battles continued in Muscat and Oman until 1976, six years after the Sultan's only son, Qaboos, who had been trained at Sandhurst, had ousted his father in a bloodless coup in which MI6 were heavily involved, advising Qaboos and providing logistics and back-up in case of any backlash. The SBS continued to assist the SAS and the Royal Marines and also acted as advisers to the Sultan's Armed Forces, as well as taking part in deep penetration missions into the desert and military operations in the mountain regions. The Ministry of Defence, however, did see the wars in Oman as a brilliant training ground for British Special Forces, honing the skills of such units as the SAS, the SBS and the Royal Marines under real-life battle conditions.

Throughout the wars in Muscat and Oman, however, the SBS had also been involved in non-stop recce operations from a new base for 6SBS (6 Troop SBS) in Malta. These recce missions were organised to uncover details of Soviet submarine capabilities, their bases and their operational capabilities, and to make accurate assessments. Britain, the United States and, of course, NATO, required detailed reports, sea charts and photographs. The only way these could be obtained with any accuracy was by clandestine methods, inserting SBS men in civilian clothes disguised as tourists or fishermen. Other SBS swimmer-canoeists would also be employed using more conventional means of acquiring the information. The operation continued for years and provided great intelligence material, enabling NATO Commanders to plan their strategy if ever Soviet submarines decided to try and break out of the Black Sea on active service.

Towards the end of the 1970s and the beginning of the 1980s, Britain's Special Forces seemed to be facing a bleak and quiet future as demands on their special qualifications were few and far between. Then, out of the blue, Argentina invaded the island of South Georgia and then the Falkland Islands and, overnight, the SAS and the SBS were back in business with a vengeance. Within hours of South Georgia being 'invaded' by Argentine scrap-metal dealers who hoisted the Argentine flag over the islands, SBS troops were scrambled and aircraft were immediately prepared to fly the troops to the scene. Ironically, in the countless books and newspaper articles written about the efforts of British forces in the South Atlantic battles of 1982, very little credit has been given to the brilliant work of the Special Boat Squadron.

First 2SBS, plus a command team, flew out to the Ascension Islands in the mid-Atlantic which would become the staging post for all British air and sea operations. There, they boarded Royal

Fleet Auxiliary Fort Austin and headed south to the icy waters around the Falklands, before being cross-decked in heavy seas and driving rain to HMS Endurance. Meanwhile, 6SBS were taken to the South Atlantic on board the nuclear-powered submarine HMS Conqueror and 3SBS went south on the slower Royal Fleet Auxiliary Stromness.

The SBS team were choppered in to Hound Bay by Wasps from HMS Endurance, taking with them heavy loads of ammunition, stores and equipment. A decision was made to gather as many SAS, SBS and Royal Marines together as quickly as possible and launch an immediate attack on the Argentine garrison of 150 men who had set up their base at Grytviken. However, there were only 75 Special Forces British soldiers available but they were confident they could take out the Argentine forces. The small British unit was landed at various points along the eastern coast of South Georgia and immediately converged on the Argentine HQ. The Argentine forces seemed surprised and overawed by the sight of British Special Forces, looking ruthless and carrying a variety of weapons, approaching them from various points, and they immediately formed up by their national flag and surrendered, putting their hands in the air. Not a single shot had been fired. For troops of the SBS, however, the capture of South Georgia was only the start of their campaign in the South Atlantic. The tough part was to follow.

As soon as the SBS troops had been relieved by more conventional British army units, they were speedily transported 900 miles north-east to the Falkland Islands. Within a matter of hours, they were being ferried and sometimes choppered to remote parts of the islands to carry out urgently needed recces. Those officers responsible for drawing up the battle plan to recapture the Falklands needed reliable first-hand information on enemy positions, the beaches that were guarded, the Argentine tactical reserves and coastal defences, gun emplacements and, most importantly, any details of land-based Exocet missile batteries.

The decision was taken to chopper in the SBS swimmer-canoeists and off-load them in remote areas, rather than trying to land them from submarines in waters which were not well chartered. It meant, of course, that the SBS soldiers had to undertake hard, long slogs across bogs and rocks to areas where it was hoped they would find satisfactory beach landing spots for the bulk of the main British force. As a result, the SBS patrols, usually made up of four-man teams, had to face long marches, staying away from their landing zones for days and nights at a time, working by night and lying low in 'scrapes' by day. They would build the scrapes by taking off the top-layer of grass or moss, scraping away a foot or so of earth, placing chicken wire over the 'scrape' and then adding the grass, making themselves virtually invisible from any patrolling aircraft. Conditions for the SBS troops were truly atrocious, often having to move across difficult terrain in cold, blinding rain while remaining vigilant for any patrolling Argentine troops.

The teams of both SBS and SAS would spend three nights away from their landing zone, carrying out their recces, and then spend two nights making tracks back to the LZ (landing zone) from where a chopper would pick them up and return them to the warmth and security of HMS Hermes. But not for long.

As D-day approached, SBS teams were choppered into San Carlos and other strategic rendezvous on the island during the hours of darkness, to set up landing lights on the beaches where the main British force would land. The work they carried out in obtaining vital detailed information for the British ground forces, the helicopter gunships and the Royal Naval gunners, played a crucial part in the swift victory that followed the landing. Indeed, two SBS squads found themselves in the centre of a fire-fight before the first attack had been made. Three SBS teams were choppered under cover of darkness into high ground above San Carlos and, as they were making their way to the landing beach, a ten-man squad of Argentine soldiers, well armed and well dug-in, barred their way to their landing zone. For ten minutes a fierce fire-fight raged but the Argentines, under the command of a young officer, refused to surrender. It was only when the officer was killed during a short, sharp SBS attack that the other soldiers surrendered and the teams were able to continue their trek to the beach.

After the British Paras had stormed ashore and had taken up positions threatening the Argentine defences, both the SBS and the SAS teams were able to move about the Falkland Islands virtually at will, unhindered by the Argentine Army. It seemed that many Argentines were so fearful of the invading British troops that they had no wish to go out on patrol and preferred to stay put in one place, defending themselves as best they could, rather than risk their lives attacking the British forces. Of course, the senior British officers realised that the great majority of the Argentine troops were young, half-trained conscripts, though the officers and NCOs were members of the regular Army. As a result, though some Argentines fought with great bravery and resistance, many had no stomach for a fire-fight. They simply wanted to get back to the mainland and safety.

But the work of the SBS and the SAS was still far from over.

The Commando Brigade had been tasked with seizing Mount Kent, the 500ft-high mountain which dominates the mountain range north-west of Port Stanley. It was the role of the SBS to ensure that the Paras and Commandos could make their way towards Stanley without fear of ambush by Argentine artillery or infantry, and they took considerable risks, scouting ahead to ensure that the main force had no unpleasant surprises. Other SBS four-man teams were choppered into the entrance of Salvador Water with their rigid raiding crafts, and then silently made their way south checking for any unwanted Argentine troops. SBS four-man teams also went ashore on West Falkland after D-day, guiding naval gunfire to their targets as well as directing Harrier jets in ground attacks, providing pin-point accurate grid reference points for Argentine machine-gun nests and camouflaged artillery sites.

The SBS even managed to establish a forward base at Volunteer Lagoon on the edge of Berkeley Sound just north of Port Stanley. And, together with SAS squads, the SBS were able to contain the 2,000 Argentine soldiers on West Falkland, making it impossible for them to break out and take part in the battle for the capital, Port Stanley.

The final flourish of the entire Falklands campaign once more involved the Special Boat Squadron and they conducted themselves with remarkable courage and professionalism under extreme conditions. The mission was to set alight the oil tanks south of the ridge across the western arm of Port Stanley harbour, but to make sure of success the SBS teams needed to infiltrate the harbour without being seen by the Argentine defenders. For two days, the SBS teams had to remain undetected as they silently steered their landing craft towards their target. But their luck, which had held good for five weeks, during which time they had evaded detection by the 8,000 Argentine troops on the island, finally failed them. As the rigid raiders crossed Stanley harbour on their way to the oil tanks, lights from a hospital ship illuminated the craft. They had two options — to continue to their target or turn and run for cover. As the Argentine forces opened up with machine-guns and mortars, the SBS raiders decided to go on and finish the task they had been set.

Within a matter of a few minutes, the four raiding craft had drawn fire from mortars, machine-guns and artillery and a few SBS men were severely wounded. The SBS scrambled ashore as planned but with more shelling and machine-gun fire directed accurately at the craft, the mission had to be abandoned. The decision was taken to rescue the wounded and these were carried five kilometres under constant fire and shelling to waiting helicopters, which flew them out to safety. The oil tanks had not been destroyed, but the raid had caused grave concern among the Argentines that the British were now within a stone's throw of Port Stanley, and victory.

The personal heroism of the SBS teams was recognised in the award of an OBE, an MBE, two

Military Medals and 12 Mentions in Despatches. Once again, the SBS had displayed professionalism and daring of the highest calibre, but very few people in Britain ever realised that the Special Boat Squadron had played such a valuable part in re-taking the Falkland Islands.

CHAPTER FOUR

The chilling statistic that all volunteers hear
shortly after they have been accepted into the
Special Boat Service is that more SBS personnel
have been killed during training and 'real-life'
exercises than in the heat of battle. And that fact
must be placed against the reality that SBS units
undertake the most dangerous missions of any
Special Forces, frequently operating behind
enemy lines. More often than not, SBS units
undertake missions in small units, against
overwhelming enemy forces, and usually within
close range of the enemy front line.

From the moment recruits join the Section,

they are taught that success and survival is in the training and the planning of operations.

'Listen, and listen carefully,' our SBS training instructor told a young corporal before operational training. 'A poorly planned mission spells disaster not just for one man but for all those taking part.' I remember hearing speeches from senior members, saying how sometimes training exercises could be more deadly, and in some cases tougher, than the real thing. Men would be injured and, God forbid, as it has happened, be killed.

As a result, I took his words of warning with a pinch of salt, as did many of my mates. We were mistaken, even foolhardy, to have done so because Operational Training with the SBS is something else.

In fact, Operational Training never ceases in the Special Boat Service, and some of the exercises we had to carry out were heartbreakingly tough. As the Royal Marines literature states when dealing with SBS recruits:

The training is within the capability of most Marines, particularly those with the mental commitment and determination to succeed.

Training is demanding, but that's the way it has to be. The rewards are most definitely worth the effort and include: a structured career; job satisfaction; realistic and challenging exercises; extra skills; training work with other Special Forces units at home and abroad; operational employment and extra pay ... but you earn it.

We all understood that for any military unit to be truly effective, regular exercises have to be made as close to real life as possible, and carried out regularly so that none of the troops become bored or too relaxed, over-confident or, heaven forbid, idle. But with reality comes a certain amount of danger and risk. We knew our instructors understood this only too well and they would always try to minimalise undue risks but, as with all potentially hazardous situations, things can and will sometimes go wrong. Even mundane, ordinary, knock-about exercises can sometimes suddenly develop into seriously dangerous situations.

The statistics from my own Royal Marines intake shows how tough the training is. Fifty young men began the 20-week basic training course at Okehampton in February 1989, and at the end of the course there were only 17 of us left. The rest had pulled out, principally as the result of injuries. Some, of course, couldn't hack the pace and the determination needed to stay the course and they either returned to their units or quit the Forces altogether.

And the training was tough, bloody tough, and the vast majority of those who had trained with me sometimes felt as I did — pissed off with the never-ending hard, physical effort which sometimes felt like torture. Looking back, it seems extraordinary how unfit I was at the start of training and it also seems extraordinary that I managed to last the course. Training for the Royal Marines isn't simply about physical fitness; it's more about commitment, an allegiance, a sense of honour imposed by every individual on himself. At the end of training one feels a great sense of achievement, bound to one's mates and the Royal Marines, as if one has taken a sworn pledge to perform one's duty as if it were a vocation. At other times, all you want to do is throw in the towel and get pissed, but something drives you on.

Occasionally, we did let our hair down and thoroughly enjoy ourselves, often getting rat-arsed in the process. During that 30 weeks of exhausting training, we were only allowed into Lympstone dressed smartly in a shirt and tie and respectable trousers. Jeans were not permitted. And before leaving camp we all had to parade in the guardroom for inspection. We hated it. We knew all the local girls would be laughing at us, looking like a bunch of prats with our short hair, walking around dressed like schoolboys when every other young guy was in jeans and open-necked shirts.

Sometimes we would rebel. We would arrange for friends outside the camp to find us fancy-dress clothes and we would change in the town. Sometimes we would walk from pub to pub dressed as Vikings with helmets, swords, smocks and Roman-type sandals. Then we became more adventurous and all dressed in nurses' uniforms with little white caps, our hairy legs showing beneath our short nurses' dresses. Generally, the girls would welcome us with open arms, buy us drinks and make a fuss because they could see we were fun blokes, out for a laugh. So successful was the nurses' dress code that we went one step further, dressing as women, wearing blouses and skirts, high-heeled shoes, stockings, make-up, lipstick and earrings. Some of my mates even shaved their legs. We even had competitions to see who was the prettiest.

But we had to keep out of the way of any NCOs or officers who frequented the pubs in Exmouth and Lympstone, so we would travel to Exeter. The girls went wild, laughing and giggling at seeing 30 or so well-built, athletic blokes walking into a pub or club for a few pints dressed up as women. The prank broke the ice immediately and many mates scored as a result, proving their masculinity!

Somehow, the instructors heard of our rebellious dress code and one morning we were all ordered to dress in PE kit and report to the parade ground. Then the training team inspected everyone's legs and those who had obviously shaved them were called all the names under the sun — from 'pansies' to 'fucking poofs'. We were all warned that, as a result, training instructors would be visiting the three towns during the evening to check that the dress code was being strictly observed.

Woe betide anyone who was seen by a training instructor dressed in anything other than shirt, tie and smart trousers. The penalty was a 'beasting' — made to run up and down the Exe estuary through deep mud until the poor bastard dropped from physical fatigue. Only then was he allowed to return to barracks for a shower. And there were other extreme physical punishments for minor misdemeanours. On one occasion, I was discovered with a small portable TV in my locker, something which was strictly forbidden. The punishment was to get dressed in full fighting order with 22lb of kit, plus a helmet and pick-axes, carrying a mate across my shoulders in a fireman's lift. He was ordered to hold two four-gallon jerry cans full of water, and I then had to run across the assault course for two hours! Every time I stopped I was ordered to get moving, the instructors yelling and screaming at me to get a move on, keep moving, run harder. It was unbelievable hell. In the end I could go no further and I simply collapsed, my heart beating madly, my muscles shaking and useless. I was absolutely knackered, exhausted to the point of fainting. It was only then that they let me go back to barracks.

Throughout our training, there was extraordinary emphasis put on physical fitness and endurance. Throughout the 26-week Royal Marines basic fitness course it was incredible how fit those that lasted the distance became. I thought I was quite fit before I began the course. Within three days, I realised how unfit I was. The marches, the runs, the assault course training, the forced marches in full fighting gear were very, very tough. Quite often I felt like jacking in the whole bloody business and going back home, but each time I felt something inside me urge me on. I don't know whether it was pride, whether I wanted to prove to myself that I could hack it with the best of them or whether it was a feeling that the instructors had instilled in all of us, a determination to succeed whatever the cost.

I will always remember the seven-day survival course on Dartmoor which was held in 40 Commando shortly after I left basic training. All élite Forces have to go through such an exercise but that doesn't make it any easier. We were each provided with a small tobacco tin in which we had to pack everything we thought we'd need. In mine, I packed some fishing twine and hooks, some flint for lighting a fire, a needle and thread, some water sterilising tablets and some condoms for carrying water. We were all impressed by the fact that a single condom will hold two litres of water.

Before being driven to Dartmoor, we were all strip-searched and anything found was confiscated. We were allowed to wear underwear and a jacket and trousers, but nothing else. No protective clothing, no poncho, nothing. The idea was that we had managed to escape capture and now we were on our own on Dartmoor with enemy troops searching for us. Split up into sections of eight, we had to march cross-country covering 14 miles every night. Then we had to search for food and lie up to avoid capture. I recall cooking nettles in the tobacco tin over a tiny fire I'd made with the flint. I also cooked worms I found in the ground. Once I found some grouse eggs which, when cooked, were delicious. On another occasion, I succeeded in catching a fish with my hook and thread but the instructor arrived at the moment I was cooking it. He took it away, telling me the fish was too nourishing.

After three days, the instructors gave us all a cereal bar and a Yorkie and told us to get on our way again. By then, most of us were feeling light-headed and dizzy, making the night-time marches really difficult. I had to concentrate simply putting one foot in front of the other. During the day, whether I found something to eat or not, I slept soundly, only waking when my stomach rumbled. What made matters worse was the fact that the training team would cook bacon and egg sandwiches for themselves right under our noses and then tease us, eating them in front of us so we could smell the delicious aroma. Most of the time I managed to smile, but towards the end I would have given my right arm for a good meal.

What kept me going, though, was the fact that I had sewn a £5 note into the inside of my boot and carefully re-stitched the thread. During the strip-search inspection no one had noticed it. During one of our night marches we passed a mobile burger van parked near a river in a car park and the following day I told the lads to keep watch as I was going to bring them back the most wonderful meal of their lives. I slipped away without the training team noticing and made my way to the burger bar, wading waist-deep about a mile-and-a-half down river. I bought as many burgers and buns, Mars Bars and cups of coffee as I could with the £5 and then returned the same way, holding the scrumptious, illicit meal well clear of the water.

I was within 100 yards of the lads when I felt someone behind me. I turned round quickly and my heart sank. Standing behind me was my Training Instructor.

'What's this then, Marine Mercer, a fucking picnic?' he asked, looking me straight in the eye.

My knees turned to jelly and I didn't know what to say. I had been caught red-handed within a few seconds of us gorging ourselves silly on the most wonderful meal we had ever had in our lives. Now we were all days away from enjoying a decent square meal. I kicked myself for not keeping a proper look-out. I kicked myself a bloody sight harder minutes later when the Instructor detailed my punishment.

'You see that boulder over there?' he asked.

'Yes, Staff,' I replied.

'And you see that hill over there?'

'Yes, Staff.'

'Well, go and pick up that boulder and run up to that hill over there and come back to me. Keep that up, at the double, until I tell you to stop. We'll see how you enjoy that picnic.'

I looked at the boulder, a bloody great thing, and then at the hill a couple of hundred yards away. I thought I might make it there and back under normal circumstances, but in my feeble state I doubted if I was up to it, let alone keep it up till he told me to stop. For a start, I could hardly pick up the boulder so two of my mates were ordered to pick it up and hand it to me.

'Right, now at the double, move,' the Sergeant shouted at me.

For 20 minutes, the bastard made me carry the boulder. To say that I ran was an exaggeration. After the first run to and from the hill I could hardly walk, I was so totally knackered. In the end, I just dropped the boulder and sat down. I couldn't move another foot. I wondered what he was going to say.

'Right, that's enough, Mercer,' he said, 'and I hope you've all learned a lesson.'

No one spoke a word, but they looked at me pityingly.

In fact, our training instructors turned out to be great guys and they won our respect. The longer that course went on, the more relaxed our instructors became. We knew in our hearts that they had to be tough, to put us through our paces. And during that time they instilled in us a sense of pride and honour to be privileged enough to wear the famous green beret of the Royal Marines. But we had to prove ourselves first.

On one occasion in June 1994, after several

weeks of tough, no-nonsense training in RIB Team SBS, our boss decided we were looking somewhat disillusioned and decided we needed a break and a little relaxation and fun. So he decided to give us a little adventure training. Because we were usually on the customary two-hour stand-by we had to take all our operational equipment with us, which was no joke. The equipment included full MCT (Maritime counter-terrorism) kit with MP5 sub-machine-guns, SIG pistols, navigation equipment, signals equipment and secure radios as well as full body armour. This was, as ever, a pain in the arse, but we accepted it as part of the job. As we were going down to Barnstaple in Devon for a whole week of rest and recuperation — a chance to let our hair down and enjoy a few gallons of beer — it was decided we should take along some RIBs (rigid inflatable boats) for practice. We knew that the seas off Devon were renowned as the best surfing beaches in southern Britain and some practice in the RIBs was always good fun.

And after we had learned to parachute — as much a necessity in the SBS as in the SAS or the Parachute Regiment — we would have great fun jumping from helicopters into the sea off the Dorset coast, particularly in the summer. We would carry out a low-level jump from a few hundred feet dressed in our black wetsuits, wearing black fins and carrying a calf knife, and then swim into the beach where we would be the centre of attention like James Bond extras walking through the summer holidaymakers sunning themselves on the beach. We would usually try to find an area where there were sufficient numbers of topless beautiful young women soaking up the sun. And we would always be surprised at the number of holidaymakers who would see us emerging from the sea and rush to take photographs. But it wasn't all about beautiful, half-naked girls desporting themselves for our pleasure. Sometimes we made mistakes.

After one night of mammoth drinking in the pubs around nearby Bideford, we had decided to go down to the beach the following morning, take out the RIBs, and practise some surf drills. We knew that this beach was renowned as a haven for nudists and we imagined that on this warm, sunny June day the beach would be dotted with beautiful, well-endowed, naked young women looking like Baywatch babes. But the reality didn't quite live up to the fantasy. I don't think I saw anyone under the age of 60 the entire day, and most seemed well into their 70s.

That day we simply took basic safety equipment — life jackets, a medical kit, safety flares and Sarbies (search and rescue beacons) and, of course, wetsuits. As we pushed out the boats, the surf was looking somewhat formidable but we thought we could quite easily cope with it. That was our first mistake. We were towed out from the shore by a World War II amphibious boat called a 'Duck' which had been used for that purpose for decades. Tom and I jumped into a 22ft RIB and the Duck headed for a piece of calm water. As soon as we were deep enough, I flashed the twin 140hp Suzuki engines, untied and floated away, waving a farewell to the Duck driver. Out past the surf it was relatively calm with just a gentle swell. However, in the line of surf the waters were savage and we jumped from wave to wave. But that was still too risky for comfort so we made a sharp turn to face the ferocious, oncoming waves. The last thing we wanted to do in front of a beach of naked oldies was to capsize the boat for we would have felt right prats. We were, after all, meant to be the crème de la crème of highly competent, well-trained Special Boat Service Marines, not incompetent beginners.

Within seconds, however, the surf swelled and we were facing 25ft-high waves pounding towards the beach and making life extremely difficult, if not downright dangerous. I knew that I had to be as delicate as possible with the throttle movement otherwise, if I revved too quickly, there was a real danger of capsizing. Tom and I glanced at each other and we didn't need to say anything. We both knew we were in dangerous waters and had to remain calm. We knew that one big wave could have flipped us over within a split second and he knew I'd seen the danger and was trying to keep the boat straight on to the waves, the only way of staying out of real trouble.

'If we can get the fuck out of this,' I shouted, 'I think we should call it a day.'

'You're on,' said Tom with a half-grin on his face. I knew that he felt the same as I did. If we had been flipped over by a wave we would probably have been OK because we were both strong swimmers and not that far from the shoreline, but we didn't want to go back to shore and admit that we had lost one of the Service's most highly sophisticated, expensive inflatables. Even worse, however, would have been the embarrassment if the tide had taken us further out

Top: With the team in Iraq, preparing for a helicopter landing.

Below: The Iraq/Turkey border – notice the bullet-holes.

Top: Honing my knife skills in Iraq!

Below: Me and a mate in the South of France, ring-riding behind an RIB.

Top: Me on an RIB, training in Northern Ireland.

Below: Getting ready for go-karting in Belfast with the lads.

Top: Me in front of a mine sweeper, Northern Ireland.

Below: Preparing for a low-level parachute jump out of a Hercules C-130.

Top: One of our team jumping from an RIB.

Below: Scooby, a sniffer dog, being hauled onto a ferry off the coast of Scotland.

Top: The *Merchant Venture* en route from Belfast.

Below: One of the *Merchant Venture* boarding crew, stood on the back of the outbound ferry.

Top: Only yards away from a deadly twister in Iraq.

Below: An SBS RIB in action.

Top: One of my team undergoing trials for fast-roping into a 20ft RIB, off the Dorset coast.

Below: SBS underway training.

to sea and it would have been necessary to call in the RAF's Search and Rescue helicopter to pluck us to safety. We would then have felt like real pricks.

Suddenly, we were hit by a really big wave which must have been about eight feet high. One engine immediately stalled making the boat almost impossible to steer. While I tried to keep the bow facing the incoming waves, Tom frantically tried to get the engine, swamped by sea water, restarted. We knew that if we stayed in the same position — riding the edge of the surf — we risked being hurled on to the beach. But we hadn't sufficient power from the single remaining engine to make it past the surf line and into calmer seas. There was only one possible escape and that was to judge the correct moment in between the waves to swing the boat around 180° and make a run towards the shore, riding the crest of a big wave. Anyone who has surfed knows that the secret of a successful run to shore is in the timing, the point at which you catch the crest of a wave at the right speed. This was much the same principle, except that I was trying to carry out the same exercise with a 22ft boat!

I shouted at Tom, telling him what I planned

to do and, of course, to prepare him for the sudden 180° spin. Then I nailed the single remaining engine, spun the boat round and headed for the shore accelerating to around 30mph. Having managed to spin the boat and catch the wave, I was now faced with the problem of beaching the rigid inflatable without wrecking it. As I was concentrating on our speed and the distance we had to travel, I hadn't noticed that groups of naked oldies had gathered on the shoreline, taking a great interest in what we were doing. I smiled briefly to myself but knew that I had to concentrate all my efforts on making sure I beached the bloody boat and didn't wreck it. I had no wish to be standing in front of some committee trying to explain how I had come to wreck a rigid inflatable while training on a Bideford beach. It wasn't exactly that we were on active service in some remote country. At the last second I cut the engine and hoped for the best as the wave took us towards the beach at twice the speed I would ever want to come ashore in an inflatable. Tom and I could only hold on and hope. For a second or two I did believe that we were going to turn turtle. Thankfully, the wave crashed around us and we were tossed on to the beach. As we came to a shuddering, sudden stop on the sand, I was thankful that we had made land and the boat had survived in one piece. But it had been more hairy than I could ever have imagined could possibly occur on a Devon beach in the middle of summer.

Only a few hours later, however, as we were relaxing and enjoying a few pints in a lovely local pub and having a laugh at the ducking we narrowly escaped, the reality of the dangers we faced were brought home to us in a dramatic and frightening way. We received a telephone call telling us that a very good mate of ours had been killed while parachuting in America's Nevada Desert, a favourite training ground for parachute jumping. Like us a few hours earlier, he, too, had been on an exercise, just practising one of the skills we had all learned in training. Neil Blain had been carrying out a full equipment free-fall practice jump from 25,000ft.

He had done nothing wrong; he had obeyed all the rules, correctly carried out all the training disciplines to the letter and yet he had bought it. After free-falling for a few thousand feet, Neil had pulled his main 'chute but, in an extraordinary million-to-one chance, the main canopy had caught on the sling attachment of the weapon he was carrying. Trained to the highest degree, Neil didn't panic. He knew precisely what to do. He pulled his main parachute release handle, which did release his 'chute, but it became entangled on the sling attachment of his M16 rifle. Like a true professional, Neil did not panic and, following correct procedure, he deployed his reserve 'chute. This 'chute unfortunately became entangled in his main 'chute, which was still streaming above his head. There was nothing else he could do. And what is so terrible, so terrifying, is that we all knew that from then on Neil would have known there was no chance of survival. He must have hurtled to earth knowing for sure that he would be killed the second he hit the ground.

The terrifying details of his death affected me greatly and for weeks afterwards I would think constantly of Neil who had been a close friend throughout our military lives together. Neil had grown up in foster homes, and the SBS and the friends he met in the unit had become his family, the family he had never known in his early life. It seemed so terribly unfair that he should die like that. He had been a damn good soldier and a good friend.

But in our way — the Royal Marines way —

we managed in some small measure to make it up to him. Whenever an SBS soldier dies, his mates hold a 'kit sale'. The same happens in the SAS and the Royal Marines, those services in which it is not unknown for men to be killed in peacetime operations or during tough operational training. The whole unit comes together and sells the dead man's kit and all the proceeds go to his immediate family to give them a helping hand. Sometimes a pair of bootlaces might sell for £50, a pair of socks for £100. It is not unknown for such sales to raise between £20,000 and £30,000, sometimes more, for the man's family. It is a wonderful tradition which brings out the very best in the unit's soldiers.

And there would be other tragedies.

'Dickie' Howard was another SBS man who died during training, killed in a freak diving accident off Portland Bill in Dorset in 1994. Dickie had been navigating a SDV (swimmer delivery vehicle) a silent, electrically driven mini-submarine used by the SBS to deliver men to their destination. Moving at a maximum of six knots, the mini-sub would arrive near its destination and the SBS men would swim away to their target. These SDVs proved invaluable when putting SBS men into strategic locations in enemy-held territory. But they are extraordinary machines. When below the surface, the subs are always full of water, making it necessary for the pilot and navigator, and anyone else in the vehicle, to wear masks. The SDVs are also incredibly difficult to control, for the pilot has only an aircraft-type joy stick, two foot pedals and a sonar device, which means that at all times the pilot is steering blind.

On this particular day, the exercise had gone really well. A safety boat was on station in case of an emergency when the SDV hit a submerged object on the sea bed. As was usual in such circumstances, the mini-sub surfaced to check for any damage but there was none and so it was decided to continue the exercise. When the mini-sub had surfaced, Dickie had taken off his face mask but the pilot, sitting next to him, didn't realise this and he dived. Unable to get his mask on properly, Dickie drowned as the sub dived to the bottom. To those of us who knew Dickie well, it seemed incredible that such a dedicated SBS man, who was superbly fit and professional, could have died in such circumstances.

And then there was my great mate, Dominic 'Salty' Salzano who died on St Valentine's Day in

1995 while undertaking 'low squares' parachuting in Norway. I felt terrible about Salty's death not only because we were close mates but because I was due to take part in that exercise myself, but couldn't make the trip so Salty volunteered to take my place. He was keen to go to Norway because he had never undergone any low-level squares parachute training, which is a vital asset for parachutists when the necessity for an accurate landing on a small drop zone is vitally important.

Our Troop Sergeant called us into the 'ready room' at our Poole headquarters and broke the terrible news. Salty had been carrying out a 'clean fatigue' jump, which meant he had been carrying no equipment whatsoever. However, incredibly, he had caught his cut-away handle as he was jumping out of the aircraft which meant that as soon as he jumped, his canopy came away. The same lever is used to operate the reserve 'chute. As he was spinning out of control and jumping from 1,500 feet, he found it impossible to release his reserve parachute and he hit the snow with no 'chute at all. He died instantly. We were all sent home.

I had never felt so awful in my life. I managed to drive home and waiting to see me was Sarah, standing at the door with a big welcome smile on her face and jokingly asking for the Valentine flowers I had promised. When she saw my face she realised something dreadful had happened. As soon as I was in the doorway, I simply broke down in tears, my body shaking with emotion, trying to come to terms with my friend's death, and finding it difficult to cope with such a devastating tragedy. Sarah was wonderful but I had never felt so miserable in my entire life. The following week I helped carry Salty's coffin at the funeral service in Liverpool, but I found it unbelievably hard to come to terms with his death.

But life had to go on and that meant more training exercises. We all understood that the need to undertake realistic training exercises is essential in the Special Boat Service because we are called upon to become closely involved in nearly all the hair-raising, dangerous real-life dramas that spring up around the world. In 1998 and 1999, the SBS found themselves involved in Kosovo and East Timor and other trouble spots which have never been revealed for diplomatic reasons. The deaths of Neil, 'Dickie' Howard and Dominic 'Salty' Salzano meant we all redoubled our efforts, pushing ourselves harder in training, putting our hearts and souls into exercises and striving to become tougher and stronger, so that others wouldn't die in some future accident.

CHAPTER FIVE

The burly, well-built Sergeant-Major looked particularly grim and ill-at-ease as he stood in front of the squad that morning explaining why he had dragged us out of bed so early and ordered an immediate parade on a cold, wet March day in Northern Ireland. He had personally walked into all the barrack rooms and ordered us out of our beds in his customary, inimitable way: 'Fucking get up and get out there. And make it sharp. This one's for real.'

We didn't need a second call. As soon as we heard and understood the urgency in his voice we were out of our beds and ready and on parade in double-quick time.

'Listen and listen well,' he said. 'There is an emergency. A suspect device has been found on Belfast's main gas supply line which passes just outside this camp. The bomb squad are already at the scene. It is our duty to get out there now and search the area for any possible terrorists who may have planted the device. We have to secure the area. We need to find those bastards, because I am telling you that if this bomb goes off, not one of us will survive, not one.'

We looked at each other wondering what the fuck he was talking about. We had never before received such an urgent and dramatic briefing. The officers and NCOs of the Royal Marines don't bullshit and dramatise events. They have respect for their men and they tell it to us straight whether it's good or bad. They've always shown that respect for the men. We knew that morning that he was being deadly serious. It's not exactly the sort of briefing you need at six o'clock in the morning when your head's still feeling fuzzy after a heavy night on the piss.

But this was Northern Ireland in the spring of 1993 and a squadron of specially trained Royal Marines were carrying out a tour of duty, playing their part in trying to bring stability and peace to a part of the United Kingdom which had been ravaged by violence, shootings and bombings for nearly 30 years. For this entire generation of the British Army, the Province of Northern Ireland had been far and away the most dangerous place in which to serve. For all, it has been a tough, dangerous assignment, not only patrolling the streets of Belfast, 'Derry and other towns, as well as bandit country, but even when off-duty enjoying a pint in a pub which could be blown apart at any moment by some Provo active service unit.

Later that day we were informed that if the bomb had gone off, our barracks in the dock would have disappeared in the blast which would have probably taken out 20 per cent of Belfast, killing thousands of innocent people. There was a further possibility that the explosion could have leapt down the pipeline, sending a ball of flame to the mainland and exploding in Liverpool, causing an enormous fireball which would have killed thousands. The damage to property would have been enormous. And all this caused by an IRA explosive device that had been attached to the main gas supply. Fortunately, the device had malfunctioned and had fallen off. I wondered if the people who had planted the device had any understanding of what would occur and how many people would have been killed and seriously burned by such an explosion.

Three hours after deploying into the surrounding area, we were told that the device had been successfully de-activated and that the task had been completed. When we moved out of camp in search of the terrorists, we knew we were being used to flush out anyone who had stayed around intent on taking pot-shots at the Security Services called in to deal with the device. The IRA often planned such evil practices, preparing booby-traps and ambushes for the Security Services who were called in to deal with suspicious packages or bombs. But, on this occasion, the bombers had primed their explosives and fled. They were never found. More importantly, the gas supply line became yet another terrorist target that had to be kept under constant surveillance.

As soon as any unit arrived in the Province, they were briefed about the importance and the dangers of both patrolling and living in Northern Ireland. To ram home the advice, maps were put up all over army barracks showing the dangerous areas which soldiers were not permitted to enter, mainly Catholic West Belfast and the Loyalist Shankill. These orders were strictly enforced and anyone found in those areas without permission was in real trouble. All serving soldiers were informed not only of the danger to which they might be exposing themselves, but also the danger to mates who might have to go in and risk their skins rescuing some stupid bastard who had not obeyed orders. Posters proclaiming 'Ignorance Is No Defence' were plastered near the tribal maps, reminding servicemen to make sure they were fully aware of the no-go areas. Anyone caught in these 'red' areas was threatened with being booted out of the Province and sent to carry out bloody awful menial tasks back at their base camp on the mainland. And no one wanted that ignominious punishment.

Before leaving our quarters in Northern Ireland, we always had to fill in a route card, stating precisely the location we intended to visit, the exact route we were taking and the estimated time of arrival. Names, rank and number of all those leaving the barracks had to be written down. We also had to give the radio frequencies we would be using on the secure radio fitted to all the vehicles we were permitted to drive while in the

Province. These cars were all provided by the Army and should have been changed every few weeks, but in fact the same cars would sometimes remain in use by servicemen for months on end. Some servicemen were highly critical of the Army's sloppy approach to our safety in not changing the vehicles more frequently, as they were directed to do, but the Ministry of Defence took no notice of those complaints. The route card was then handed in to the duty officer and checked before the servicemen were allowed to venture out.

Whenever any personnel left barracks in Northern Ireland, personal weapons were always carried. Most of us carried a Heckler & Koch MP5 plus a 9mm Browning. Some mates took SA80s for greater fire-power if we ended up in an ambush. We would also carry a car bag, containing medical kit and, more importantly, smoke grenades. And before leaving base we would discuss our 'action-on' procedure, going over what we planned to do if confronted with an unforeseen emergency such as a puncture, a car crash, a road accident or if we came under attack. We all knew exactly what to do, how to react and what action to take. One of our regular training exercises, which we would practise on the firing ranges, was escaping from an ambush set up on the road.

This would entail driving along and suddenly coming under fire, usually from an IRA road-block thrown up in bandit country in South Armagh. If the Provo Active Service Unit (ASU) opened fire then our driver would slam on the brakes, ram the car in reverse, and do a 'J' turn while the guy in the passenger seat would open up, through the windscreen if necessary, aiming directly at the gunmen. The driver would then reverse as fast as he could, swing the car round and head off back the way we had come while the other guy in the vehicle would continue to return fire.

'Contact … Wait … Out' were the three words the other passenger would flash over the car's secure radio, alerting the Operations Room that we were under fire. As soon as possible, a report would be sent to the Ops Room telling them precisely what had occurred and giving the map references of the IRA ambush position so that if a decision was taken to follow up the contact, the patrol would have all the necessary information. Choppers would be scrambled in an effort to hunt down the gunmen and, on occasions, a four-man SBS/SAS squad might be choppered into the immediate vicinity.

A similar, less dramatic alert would be radioed in if an accident occurred or the car got a puncture, so that the Ops Room was always aware of what was going on and the exact location of the vehicle. It was a necessary and very sensible precaution which, as far as I know, was always followed to the letter.

However, on one occasion, my Royal Marine mate Brian and I got lost. We had only been in Northern Ireland a couple of weeks and were driving to see some pals who were living in barracks near Aldergrove Airport. We had been given a Ford Sierra and had filled out a route card and handed it in as required. Brian was driving and I was navigating when we came across an RUC check-point. Brian produced his driving licence and the RUC officer said there had been a device found on the road ahead and told us to make a detour. That's when we got lost.

Suddenly I said to Brian, 'We're in the fucking Shankill.'

'Don't talk daft,' Brian replied, 'we're miles from the Shankill.'

'Well, if we're miles from the Shankill, why

does the sign on that building read "Shankill Community Centre"?'

'Oh shit,' he said, 'this area's out of fucking bounds. If anything goes wrong here we will really be in the shit either from the Loyalists or from the Officers when we get back to base.'

I was feverishly checking the map to find the best way out of the Shankill and the quickest route to Aldergrove. I had never been in the Shankill before and I was amazed at the condition of the place; the run-down houses and shops, the scarred buildings, the burned-out cars lying around the place and the apparent poverty of many of the people. But I was impressed by the huge amount of carefully painted Loyalist graffiti on the sides of houses and buildings. I had envisaged the Shankill being a smart, middle-class area but this appeared poor and derelict, almost abandoned. When we finally left the Shankill and arrived at Aldergrove, we certainly enjoyed that first pint. It took a pint or two to calm our nerves but it had taught us a lesson — to make bloody sure we knew exactly where we were at all times when driving around Belfast. Back at base, we told no one of our adventure.

Some months later, a Protestant civilian mate

of mine who worked at Moscow Barracks invited me to his home for tea and I knew he lived in a safe Protestant area of Belfast which was virtually untouched by the Troubles. I agreed to go, thinking it would be great to have tea with a civilian family in their home away from the barracks and army life.

As we were driving through Belfast, he suddenly said, 'Let's stop and have a pint, I'm dying for a drink.'

'Will it be all right?' I asked, sounding a little pathetic.

'Of course it will,' he said, 'this is my local, all my mates drink here. No need to worry, this is the Shankill.'

That one word put the fear of God in me and I wondered what the hell he was doing bringing me to the Shankill, an area he knew was out of bounds to any army personnel when off duty. For a second I wondered if this chap, my mate, was in reality a hard-line Loyalist. But I dismissed that thought because I had known him for some months and he had always been a good friend. In fact, he didn't seem to have any particular allegiance to the Loyalist cause.

We hadn't been in the crowded bar more

than a couple of minutes when my mate turns round and says in a loud voice so the whole bar could hear, 'This is Pete, my Royal Marine mate.'

I could have died. I turned white and looked at him in astonishment.

'Cheers,' he said, a big smile on his face, and took a large gulp from his pint.

Not wanting to seem scared out of my wits, I somewhat feebly replied 'Cheers' and took about four gulps from my pint, almost finishing it.

'You're thirsty,' he said, and went to the bar to buy me another.

I looked around the room and noticed what I recognised as bullet holes along one of the walls.

'What are those?' I asked, hoping I had made a mistake.

'Bullet holes,' he replied cheerfully.

'How often has this pub been attacked?' I asked.

'Only a couple of times,' he said blithely, still sounding cheerful. 'Listen,' he continued, 'I know you're in the Marines but take a tip from me. If the door comes flying open it'll be the IRA. Just dive for the floor and try to find some cover. OK?'

'Fuck me,' I replied, 'I thought we were

dropping in here for a quiet pint, not a fucking gun battle.'

'Don't worry,' he said, trying to calm my nerves, 'it's been months since the IRA attacked this bar.'

Surreptitiously, I tapped the top of my trousers, reassuring myself that I had my 9mm Browning concealed there and checked that I was carrying two full clips of ammunition giving me 26 rounds. I also had my secure radio with me, hidden under my jacket. Gradually I began to relax and enjoyed a couple more pints before leaving and having tea at my mate's home with his wife and three kids, which I really enjoyed. But I breathed a great sigh of relief when he dropped me back at barracks three hours later.

But there were occasions when the Royal Marines were called into action against the Provos. Perhaps the most famous occasion was in 1991 when a section of eight Marines from 45 Commando were holed up in a sangar overlooking a small town in South Armagh. They had received an intelligence report from a reliable source that a Provo ASU planned to attack the sangar with RPGs (rocket-propelled guns), the ones capable of taking out a main battle tank. We knew that if a sangar was hit by an RPG, the effect would be horrendous, tearing the building apart and probably killing a number of its occupants. Two nights before the expected attack, another troop of 24 men from 45 Commando were choppered into the sangar to reinforce the place and provide back-up if an attack was launched. The Army was convinced that its intelligence was good and it wanted to be ready for the attack.

It was while the men from 45 Commando were having their evening meal dressed in fatigues and ready for action that the 'ping-ping' sound of rounds hitting metal was heard. The men knew that meant the sangar was under attack because they recognised the noise instantly. Everyone leapt into action, racing to pick up their 'fighting order' which comprised weapons, ammunition, helmets, body armour and a belt containing basic rations, water and a lightweight poncho, before gathering at the pre-arranged spot towards the rear of the sangar. The look-out confirmed that a group of armed men were about 100 yards away, coming up the hill towards the sangar, occasionally stopping to fire off a few rounds. He did not report that he had seen an RPG, but he guessed they would try to conceal the weapon to surprise them at a later stage of the gun battle.

'On the count of three,' shouted the Troop Sergeant, 'bomb burst out of the sangar.'

He didn't have to wait for a reply. Everyone knew the drill.

'One … two … three,' and the men of 45 Commando burst out of the sangar and scattered.

'Look and locate the enemy,' shouted the Sergeant and everyone all took up positions as the Provos scattered, surprised by the Marines' tactics. The Provos had expected the troops inside the sangar to stay put and open fire from within the building and not to come rushing out to confront them. The Marines had taken them by surprise.

Suddenly from above, the sentries on top of the sangar opened fire on the Provo gunmen with their powerful GPMG (general purpose machine-gun) laying down an awesome field of fire around the spot where they had last seen the Provos.

Then, under the direction of the Troop Sergeant, the Marines began to put down well-organised offensive fire, everyone taking careful aim and firing single shots with their SA80 rifles which were equipped with night sights and thermal-imaging devices. Charlie and Delta teams took it in turns to open fire, taking their orders from the Troop Sergeant who was in charge of the gun battle.

Then everything went quiet.

'Advance to contact,' came the order from the Sergeant, and Charlie and Delta teams took it in turns to advance, take cover and wait for the other team to pass through them. This went on as 45 Commando continued down the hill towards the town, only opening fire if they saw a man running. Overhead, however, the chatter of the GPMG hardly ever ceased, which must have created alarm among the Provo gunmen. Those machine-guns can lay down extraordinary fire making it extremely difficult for an enemy to do anything except take cover and lie low. But the IRA had to get out of their predicament and had no option but to break cover and retreat into the town. If they stayed to fight it out they didn't stand a chance. They would all have been wiped out. Only when 45 Commando reached the edge of the town did they stop firing and re-group and the machine-gun ceased its incessant chatter.

Traces of fresh blood were on the road and the commandos knew they must have hit at least one of the Provos. It was confirmed later that the next day two bodies were delivered to a hospital south of the border and two wounded men were treated for gunshot wounds. When 45 Commando returned to the sangar, an urgent message was sent back to headquarters demanding a re-supply of ammunition. The machine-guns alone had fired 1,500 rounds that evening and every Marine had fired between 60 and 100 rounds, amounting to a couple of thousand rounds. It was the only time in the last 30 years of fighting the IRA in Northern Ireland that any unit had ever had to have an ammunition re-supply as a result of a contact.

It was the last action by 45 Commando during that tour of duty in the Province and they were then sent on a week's leave. Some had booked flights to Spain and the Canary Islands, others to Florida. But they never made it out of Britain. Some of 45 Commando were actually sitting on aircraft waiting to fly out on holiday when airline representatives came on board and ordered all the Marines off the plane, telling them they had to report to base. Recalled immediately to camp, they were given the news that 45 Commando were to spearhead the Commando Brigade in Northern Iraq. It was the start of Operation Haven, an integral part of the Gulf War.

For the most part of the Operation I was on in Northern Ireland I was tasked with stopping and searching the ferries running back and forth from Larne and Belfast to the mainland. The intelligence services knew these ferries were constantly used by members of the IRA and the Loyalist paramilitaries for moving people, guns and ammunition. We spent much of our time patrolling both Carlingford Lough near the Mountains of Mourne and, on occasions, Strangford Lough, with its wonderful bird sanctuary. There was also the vast inland waterway of Lough Neagh which was one of the most popular routes used by Republicans and Loyalists to ferry arms, ammunition and personnel from point to point, away from the danger of police and army check-points which, at a moment's notice, could be thrown up across roads all over the Province.

Searching the ferries was, of course, our prime occupation. We employed powerful, twin-engined RIBs to ferry us around the loughs. We would take up a discreet hiding-place somewhere along the lough and emerge shortly after the targeted ferry had passed by. Within a matter of minutes, we would be alongside the ferry and over the radio the Captain would be ordered to slow down and, if necessary, stop engines. We would then send a boarding party up the grappling ladders to carry out a stem to stern search of the boat. We were always armed and generally speaking quite a frightening force, dressed in black wet suits and balaclavas and carrying guns. But we tried to be as friendly as possible to the passengers, especially the youngsters.

If there was a suspicion of explosives on board, we would take Scooby, our Springer spaniel, with us, hauling him up the 35ft from our RIB to the deck in a special harness. But Scooby, though brilliant at his task of sniffing out firearms and explosives, simply hated being put in a harness and hauled up the side of the ferry. In fact, he so loathed the operation that half-way up he would become so frightened he would shit over everyone in the RIB below. We quickly learned never to stand beneath poor old Scooby but would always give the job of sending Scooby on deck to a new member of the team who had just joined the patrol. We never told the new guy the danger he was facing which frequently caused much hilarity, except for the poor bastard who found himself covered in excrement.

In reality, it seemed to us that both the IRA and the Loyalists had quickly discovered that we constantly raided the passenger ferries for we never made any significant finds during the months I was there. However, a few passengers were arrested during our searches and taken away for questioning, but I had no idea what happened to them.

In the early 1990s, however, a new specially designed fast patrol boat was introduced specifically for the purpose of chasing and boarding the boats carrying paramilitary personnel and guns which quietly and without lights criss-crossed Lough Neagh almost on a nightly basis. Those little boats, purportedly fishing smacks, would carry men wanted by Special Branch or weapons of all descriptions. The 40ft-long boat was covered in tough, bullet-proof Kevlar, and boasted a brand-new, revolutionary thermal imaging device. For years, of course, such imaging devices had been employed by the RUC, the British Army and the Royal Navy. But this particular one not only managed to pinpoint an individual but could also track the person along a shore, or through a wooded area, making it all but impossible for the person under surveillance to escape.

We would then contact one of our shore patrols which would home in and make an arrest. The revolutionary high-tech device was so pin-point accurate that it could even pick up a rabbit a few hundred yards away and follow it along the shoreline.

The boats themselves, powered by twin engines, were floating arsenals carrying an armed SBS team. These vessels proved great fun and very popular with the lads because they were such a great boon to our job. We had the speed, the fire-power and the imaging device capable of tracking personnel for miles without their knowledge.

We also enjoyed our billeting arrangements during those months we spent patrolling the loughs for we took over a picturesque, rose-covered, brick-built fishermen's cottage which was about 100 years old. It was small but had the necessary basics of a bathroom, three bedrooms, a living room and a kitchen and we loved staying there. One reason for that cottage becoming so popular was the fact that it was only a stone's throw from the bar on the lough where both the SAS and the SBS personnel used to drink when off duty. They were the times, far from civilisation, when having the odd drink or two was the only recreational activity we could enjoy. We would get fed-up watching TV non-stop, listening to the radio or records or reading books and magazines.

One dangerous occupational hazard that many servicemen encountered in Northern Ireland was the constant threat of the accidental discharge of weapons. Because of the inherent danger to one and all, such negligent discharges were always treated very seriously and anyone found guilty of being responsible faced a heavy fine. The Royal Marines took pride in the fact that we were so professionally trained we would never be so stupid as to commit the cardinal sin of a negligent discharge. But, of course, on occasions it did happen. Because most of the soldiers in Northern Ireland were using live ammunition on a daily basis, the odds were that, on occasions, some bastard would make a mistake and fire off a round. If ever a round was discharged accidentally in a building, the drill was to hit the deck as quick as lightning because the round would fly around the room, bouncing off the walls and ceiling, and the floor was considered the safest place. And there must have been more than a score of incidents of soldiers being injured, some seriously, by such accidents. There were, however, some discharges which, though dangerous, were also very funny, and which would give us a laugh for weeks.

One of the funniest incidents occurred when we were on duty in the Province, living in the fisherman's cottage near Lough Neagh. One spring night in 1993, we had just returned from a patrol with RUC officers and were having a couple of late-night pints in the bar not far from the cottage which was situated inside a security fence. We had checked our weapons into the armoury when we heard what sounded like the firing of a pistol. We thought nothing of it and presumed someone had been clearing a weapon.

A few minutes later, an RUC officer came into the bar and confessed that he had accidentally discharged his 9mm Browning while cleaning it in the kitchen of the cottage. Apparently, he had cocked the Browning before taking the magazine out, putting a round up the spout. When he checked the weapon by firing it into the air, the pistol had gone off, puncturing a hole in the ceiling.

'Did anyone hear you?' someone asked.

'I don't know,' replied the RUC officer, 'but no one's been round to check. Hopefully no one heard anything.'

'Well, you're fucking lucky,' someone told him, 'otherwise you would have been heavily fined.'

'I know,' he replied, 'what should I do with the hole in the ceiling? Someone might notice.'

'Stuff some lavatory paper in it, no one will notice,' someone suggested.

'Right,' he said, and within five minutes he had returned, the job safely carried out.

As we continued drinking, Dave, one of my mates, turned to me and asked, 'Where's Mike, the Royal Navy signaller?'

'He went off to sleep,' I replied. 'He was off-duty and spent the day drinking himself into a stupor. He went to sleep it off. Why do you ask?'

'Fuck me,' said Dave, 'I've just been thinking. You know that round the RUC fella fired off? Well, Mike sleeps in the bedroom above the kitchen. I wonder if he's OK.'

Four of us raced from the room, ran across the grass and up the stairs of the cottage. As we ran, I envisaged poor Mike lying dead in his bed, shot by the stupid cop. We burst into his room but he was out cold, oblivious to the noise and snoring away like some old goat. I went to check him and, for some unknown reason, pulled back the blankets. My mouth dropped open. The bed was soaked in blood, fresh blood.

'Shit, look at this,' I said.

'Fuck,' someone said, 'we had better wake him.'

'But carefully,' someone else said, 'he might die of shock. I wonder what the fuck happened.'

'But why didn't he wake up? Is he conscious?' someone else asked.

'Of course he's fucking conscious,' I said, 'he's snorting away like an old pig.'

'Wake him gently,' advised someone else. 'Just put the covers back over him and then wake him and tell him what's happened.'

So we shook him and shook him again but it was obvious he was enjoying a real drunken sleep.

'We've got to wake him,' I said, 'he'll need a blood transfusion looking at this lot.'

Finally, we woke him and told him there had been an accident.

'What the fuck are you talking about?' Mike said grumpily. 'What the fuck's going on?'

'We think you've been shot,' someone said.

'Shot? Shot? What the hell's going on?' he said.

'Take a look, mate,' someone said and peeled

back the covers.

'Shiiiit!' he yelled. 'What the fuck …?'

'You've been shot,' I said.

'Christ,' he said, 'it fucking looks like I've been butchered!'

When we examined Mike, we discovered that the RUC man's bullet had gone through the mattress, and through both of his thigh muscles. Luckily, the bullet had missed the femur, but the blood from the flesh wounds was everywhere. We got a medic and Mike was taken to hospital. Ten days later, he was discharged from hospital and had to return to the mainland to recuperate fully. When he rejoined the unit again, he was given an awful ribbing. We really took the piss out of him. No one could recall anyone ever being shot through both legs while asleep and not waking up. The wretched RUC man received a heavy fine.

For the great majority of the weeks and months we spent patrolling the lochs of Northern Ireland, the lads of the Marines and the matelots of the Royal Navy got on famously together. When off duty, we would often have a few beers together. To be fair, there wasn't exactly much to do on board a boat, surrounded by land where the Provos reigned supreme, and which we called bandit country. If we didn't have the occasional drink in the mess, all we could do was sit around watching TV or reading.

But there was nearly a mutiny on board an ex-Royal Navy minesweeper during Christmas 1992 when the skipper banned the Marines and the matelots from having any drink whatsoever. To us, that seemed a stupid decision because the Skipper should have known that Royal Marines love a drink when off duty and this was Christmas. Three Marines had discovered that one of the ship's officers was carrying a loaded 9mm Browning around the boat while on duty. We knew that he was perfectly entitled to walk around with the Browning, but not a loaded one. An argument developed between the First Officer and two of our NCOs.

The officer told our NCOs, 'I am entitled to carry a weapon while on duty. And if I decide it should be loaded, then that is my prerogative.'

'No, it isn't,' he was told. 'It's against orders, unless the ship is under attack or under threat of an attack.'

'I make the decisions here,' he replied, 'the matter is at an end, do you understand?'

One of our NCOs, named JT, turned to leave

but suddenly turned back, grabbed the officer's Browning and forcibly wrenched it out of his hand before he realised what was happening.

'Give me back that weapon at once,' shouted the angry officer.

'No,' JT replied, 'you have behaved irresponsibly. I'm confiscating it.'

'I am an officer. You must obey me.'

'I don't care who the fuck you are,' replied JT. 'You're not having the weapon back again. I'll hand it to the skipper and tell him why I had to confiscate it.'

The skipper had no option but to accept that what JT had done was correct in that instance but he hated the idea that an NCO had overruled one of his senior officers in that way. The skipper tried to hush up the incident but the Marine NCOs requested that an example should be made of the officer because of the inherent danger in permitting anyone to walk around a ship with a loaded weapon. The skipper didn't like that one jot but realised he had no option but to report the matter to a higher authority. However, it was not the end of the matter.

The skipper ordered a total ban on all alcohol over the Christmas period, whether we were on or off duty. He maintained that alcohol could lead to a lack of military discipline and, as the Royal Naval vessel was active over the Christmas period he considered it better if no alcohol was permitted. We argued that all servicemen in the Royal Navy, Army and Air Force were permitted to drink on Christmas Day, and we were also entitled to do so. Still he refused. We didn't like that, we didn't like that one fucking bit!

We held a council of war trying to find a way of getting around the skipper's stupid ban. Then someone had a bright idea. On board was a highly accurate satellite navigation system which could pin-point dots on the map with remarkable accuracy. We decided to employ it to make sure we didn't have a dry Christmas. Firstly, we contacted our mates who were patrolling along the loch shores using our secure military ship-to-shore radio. We asked them to find an off-licence outlet, buy three packs of 24 cans of Heineken and place the booze at an exact spot in a few feet of water on the edge of the loch. A day later, when some lads took out a rigid raider to patrol the loch, they stopped at the spot and immediately found the Heineken. It was a simple operation to smuggle it aboard the minesweeper.

As Christmas approached we had discussions about what we should do. We knew the skipper had no intention of lifting the no-alcohol ban but we had not only the Heineken but also four litres of dark, navy rum, which we could drink as chasers.

As someone said, 'Fuck it. We may as well be hung for a sheep as a lamb. Let's get the booze, barricade ourselves in the Mess for the whole of Christmas Day, and have a piss-up.'

'But that's mutiny,' someone suggested.

'No it isn't,' someone countered. 'We're off duty. All we're doing wrong is disobeying the skipper's stupid ban.'

The idea was greeted with enthusiasm and early on Christmas Day we all trooped into the Mess with our booze and barricaded ourselves in by banging home the eight clips that secure the watertight door in case of emergency. Now there was no way anyone could dislodge us until we decided to come out and face the music. And we had no intention of doing that until all the booze had gone. In fact, we stayed there eight hours, drinking, singing, listening to music and watching television. The skipper went mental, banging on the door, ordering us to open the door, and threatening us with dire consequences if we didn't obey his orders. We just turned up the music and continued drinking until we were all happily pissed — and couldn't care a damn what action the skipper took against us.

The following day we were all commanded to attend Captain's orders. But there was a problem. We had no uniforms on board except for our 'woolly bear' suits, which we wore under our black wetsuits to keep us warm in winter. They were thermal, woolly-looking, one-piece suits which covered the whole body except for the head, hands and feet. So we trooped in line to the bridge looking absolutely stupid in our woolly suits and wearing flip-flops on our feet and our smart SBS berets on our heads. The other officers on the bridge that morning were having great trouble preventing themselves bursting out laughing. As the skipper addressed us we could hear the other officers giggling in the background. The Captain charged two of our lads with being drunk and disorderly and fined them £80 each. The rest of us were given an official reprimand. We explained that we were only having fun, that we were all off duty and that it was Christmas Day. But the unfortunate incidents meant that the crew on board his vessel had lost regard for the skipper and that was not a good state of affairs on board a ship. Within a few months, however, the skipper was transferred to another ship. Some of our mates thought we had been bloody lucky to escape with only a reprimand because technically we could have been charged with the most heinous crime on the high seas — mutiny.

CHAPTER SIX

One warm, sunny May afternoon in New York in 1972, an unknown caller telephoned the owners of the QEII liner and asked to speak to the man in charge. Reluctantly, Charlie Dickson, Cunard's operations director, agreed to take the call. That phonecall began one of the most dramatic peacetime escapades in the history of the SBS and, as a result of that single incident, the Special Boat Service introduced one of the most dangerous training exercises practised regularly by the unit.

'Listen carefully,' said the man, who spoke with an American accent. 'There are a series of six bombs that have been placed aboard the QEII, hidden in places where you will never find them and on various decks. These bombs will explode while the ship is at sea unless $350,000 is handed over tomorrow.'

Charlie Dickson began to try and find out more about the threat, playing for time, trying to gather more information from the stranger, but he cut him off in mid-sentence.

'Listen to me,' the caller went on, 'I have two accomplices on board the ship and they don't care if they live or die. One is an ex-con, the other a man dying of cancer. These men will detonate the bombs at a given time unless the cash is handed over by tomorrow.'

Again Dickson tried to intervene, to find out anything he could about the man and his two accomplices, anything in fact that might help the police or the FBI trace the men and find the bombs. Dickson knew better than anyone that at that moment the QEII was sailing from New York to Cherbourg, and then to Southampton, with 1,438 passengers on board as well as 850 crew.

Again, the mystery caller intervened. 'Listen carefully,' he said again. 'I will make contact later so that we can make arrangements where you should drop the money. Make sure you get it, all of it, and also be warned that under no circumstances must you contact the police. Remember, if we don't get the money your famous QEII will be blown out of the water.'

Then he hung up.

Within minutes, Dickson had called Richard Patton, President of Cunard North America. He called in the New York Police Department who alerted the FBI. Their advice was to treat the ransom demand seriously. The FBI advised an immediate search of the ship without alerting the passengers. They also advised Cunard to arrange the immediate withdrawal of the $350,000 in cash and make it available for the drop, as the caller had demanded. The FBI cautioned Cunard to act on the basis that bombs were on board and that they would be exploded if the money was not paid over. Cunard's directors agreed to carry out the FBI's advice to the letter. After all, they were experts at dealing with such demands and threats.

A coded wire message was sent to the QEII's master, Captain William Law, a calm, experienced 60-year-old, informing him of the ransom demand and ordering a search of the ship without alerting the passengers to the dangers. Captain Law was fully aware that searching for the bombs on the ship would be like looking for the proverbial needle in a haystack, but he called in his officers and told them to alert the crew and informed them in the strictest secrecy exactly what was going on. He also ordered the ship to be searched from stem to stern, but discreetly.

On shore, passenger lists were being examined by Special Branch officers looking for anything suspicious, and the list was also wired to the FBI so that they, too, could investigate the passengers. All ship-to-shore telephone calls were also monitored. On advice, the Ministry of Defence in London was informed of the threat and, within minutes, Prime Minister Edward Heath was told. The Ministry of Defence alerted both the SAS and the SBS, as well as the Royal Army Ordnance Corps (RAOC) bomb-disposal unit. There was, of course, no one on board the ship capable of dealing with unexploded bombs and so it became imperative to find a way of putting bomb disposal experts on to the QEII while the ship was in mid-Atlantic.

Two hours after the phonecall had been made to Cunard's New York office, Lieutenant Jack Cliff and Corporal Keith Johnson were on their way by helicopter from SBS headquarters at Poole to RAF Lyneham. A C130 Hercules was on the tarmac being prepared for take-off. Also joining them on the flight was Flight-Sergeant Alex Smith, the SBS parachute jump instructor, and Flight-Sergeant Jeffrey Bauldrey who had been called in to train the RAOC bomb-disposal expert, Captain William Jones. For there was one major problem which had to be overcome during the three-hour flight to the QEII: Captain Jones had had virtually no parachute training, and had never in his life parachuted into cold, rough seas!

When the C130 was 30 minutes from the drop zone, the four men began pulling on their dry suits. The plan was for Corporal Johnson and Sergeant Oliver Mackenzie to jump, taking with them the bulk of the bomb-disposal gear, while Lieutenant Cliff would jump with Captain Jones and talk him through the drills as they parachuted together from the Hercules. It was also his task to ensure that the bomb-disposal expert did not drown when they hit the water. Captain Jones was given a PX4 parachute, one which had to be unbuckled when 200 feet above the water so that he would not be dragged beneath the waves by the weight of the wet parachute when he landed.

Throughout the drill, Captain Jones had been

looking decidedly nervous. After he had pulled on his dry suit and the 'chute had been placed on his back, he said, 'I must tell you; I feel bloody awful.'

The experienced parachutists looked at each other, fearful that the drop could go terribly wrong and mindful of the fact that Captain Jones was the most important person in the entire operation. If he didn't make it aboard the QEII the mission would have been a terrible waste of time, and it could have tragic and devastating consequences.

'Don't worry,' he was told, 'we all feel like this before the first jump into water. Really, it's a piece of cake.'

He looked at them, knowing they were trying to cheer him up, but he realised this jump would be no piece of cake. 'I believe you,' he said with a half-smile on his face, 'but I do feel bloody awful. And I feel sick.'

While the Hercules was still some distance from the ship, Captain Law decided that the time had come to tell the passengers what was happening. At 2.20pm he announced over the loudspeaker system, 'I have an announcement to make. We will shortly be taking procedures to check a report that there may be a bomb on board. We have already conducted a search of the ship and found nothing. The likelihood is fairly remote … However, we have to be certain. Very shortly we will be receiving the assistance of British bomb-disposal experts, who will be circling above us in RAF aircraft. They will be dropped into the sea and will be brought aboard. In the meantime, please try not to alarm yourselves.'

The passengers immediately returned to their cabins to collect their cameras and the decks quickly became crowded as everyone gathered to watch the unfolding drama. It wasn't every day that ocean liners were visited by parachutists searching for unexploded bombs!

What the passengers didn't know, however, was that in New York the mystery man had been in touch with Cunard's offices once more. But this time he didn't phone; he sent a hand-written letter by special delivery ordering Charlie Dickson to place the $350,000 in $10 and $20 bills in a blue canvas bag and proceed to a particular telephone booth on Route 299, a two-hour drive from New York. There, Dickson would be given further instructions.

The note added, 'You will be watched. Be alone. Any sign of police and you will have a catastrophe on your hands. Remember Hong

Kong.' This was a reference to the old Queen Elizabeth liner which had burned out in Hong Kong harbour in 1971.

The note continued, 'You must arrive at the telephone booth at 9.30pm. If anything goes wrong, the ship will blow within the hour.'

There was also a serious, life-threatening drama going on in the Atlantic as the Hercules pilot discovered that the cloud cover was so low it had become dangerous for the parachutists to jump at such low altitude, only 700 feet above the water. But they had to make that jump. There was no question of aborting the mission. First, Keith Johnson and Oliver Mackenzie hurled themselves out of the port side with all the equipment, but Captain Jones and Lieutenant Cliff had to wait for two more runs before it was possible for them to follow.

Above the noise of the Hercules engines and the wind, the two Flight-Sergeants were screaming last-minute instructions to the hapless Jones who looked as white as a sheet as he waited for the order. As the Hercules circled for the second run, Captain Jones became violently sick.

Sixty seconds later, the Flight-Sergeants and Cliff yelled 'Go' at the top of their voices and

Jones, with Cliff seconds behind, threw themselves out of the aircraft door. As he landed awkwardly in the water, Jones disappeared under the heavy waves and Cliff began searching for him. But, finally, after 20 seconds or more, he surfaced and Cliff swam over to him to check whether he was all right. The wretched Captain was still feeling sick and seemed to have little strength, so Lieutenant Cliff held him above the waves until the QEII's lifeboat had chugged to the scene and picked them up. On deck, the enthusiastic passengers were filming every second of the drama, elbowing each other out of the way in their efforts to find a good spot from which to film the action. Fortunately, Jones had not been injured in the jump, but he did still feel bloody awful.

In New York, Charlie Dickson had driven to the appointed telephone booth while FBI agents, in unmarked vehicles, drove around the area. Ten minutes after the agreed time, when Dickson had begun to think the whole thing was a hoax, the phone rang and he picked up the receiver. Dickson immediately recognised the caller's voice.

'I told you not to call in the police,' said the mystery man.

'So?' replied Dickson.

'But you did call them. I know they are there with you,' replied the caller.

'Well,' stammered Dickson, not sure how to reply.

'Well,' said the caller, 'you have now put the lives of everyone on board that ship at risk.'

'I had no choice,' replied Dickson, 'the Board of Directors insisted. Cunard is a public company and I had to reveal the truth to the directors to get the money.'

'Well, listen carefully once more,' said the caller, 'and this time make sure you follow my instructions precisely. OK?'

'Yes, OK,' said Dickson.

'Now listen,' said the man. 'Drive to the diner 200 yards down the road. Park and go straight to the washroom. You will find a message taped to the underside of a wash basin. And don't try anything clever; there will be three guns trained on your every move.'

'Right,' replied Dickson, wondering whether he should have taken the advice of the FBI and let an agent take his place, pretending to be him.

Dickson carried out the caller's instructions, finding the diner, the washroom and the message beneath the basin. The note instructed him to drive down the road to a deserted spot a few hundred yards away. There he would find a marker where he should leave the bag containing the money. Once it had been received without incident, a call would then be made to the QEII to defuse the bombs.

Dickson did as he was instructed and, after leaving the bag next to the marker he drove back to New York leaving the FBI to keep watch. The mystery caller never approached the bag of money. On board the QEII, searches for the bombs continued, but none were ever discovered. During the two-day voyage to Cherbourg, however, the four parachutists were treated like VIPs, given first-class accommodation and entertained lavishly by the passengers for risking their lives parachuting into the heavy seas. As soon as the ship docked at Cherbourg, the bag of money was picked up and handed back to Cunard. The ship was thoroughly searched once again but nothing was found, and the mystery caller never called Cunard again.

The four parachutists were all awarded the Queen's Commendation for Bravery. More importantly, however, Government Ministers, Ministry of Defence planners and senior officers quickly came to the realisation that luxury liners were an easy target for terrorist groups wanting to promote their causes by appearances in world headlines. The early 1970s was a time of burgeoning international terrorist activity, particularly by the Palestinians, the German Baader-Meinhof gang, Basque separatists and the IRA. On this occasion, those passengers on the QEII had been fortunate that it had only been a hoaxer at work. If a terrorist organisation had put six or seven gunmen on board, purporting to be passengers, and then made their demands, the British Government and security chiefs would have been in an impossible position. They would have been unable to refuse the terrorists' demands without putting the lives of hundreds of innocent passengers and crew at risk.

The hoax on the QEII happened to occur at the moment that the first oil from the North Sea was being pumped from the ocean bed and it had become obvious that the North Sea oil bonanza would require the building of scores of massive oil rigs to withstand the huge seas off the North of Scotland. These rigs might also have become a target for terrorist groups closer to home. As a result, the decision was taken that the SBS, as well as the SAS, should be trained, as a matter of urgency, in storming terrorist-controlled oil rigs, as well as ships at sea.

As a result, all SBS personnel have since been trained to parachute into rough seas with heavy gear, taking with them high-powered RIBs and all the necessary equipment, including various weapons, secretly climbing on to ships and liners of all sizes and then, if necessary, eliminating ruthless terrorists who know for certain that the SBS will shoot first and ask questions later. It is, in fact, one of the most dangerous training exercises undertaken by SBS personnel, simply because of the inherent danger in jumping into rough ocean seas from low-flying aircraft and then clambering on to a super liner moving at perhaps 25 knots through the water. The danger during such exercises is being pulled beneath the stern and drowned or, even worse, finding oneself sucked into the huge propellers churning below the surface.

In December 1994, I was thrilled but nervous to discover that I had been selected for a QEII training exercise. And this was to be the 'Full Monty' with all of M Squadron SBS taking part and two teams from Red Troop SAS. On ship-storming exercises we would sometimes use rubber weapons, the same size and weight as real ones, so that our real weapons weren't ruined by immersion in sea water, which rapidly shortens their lifespan. However, on this particular exercise we were to use real weapons with blank rounds and four 22ft-long RIBs with twin engines. The three SBS teams and one SAS team would be in the RIBs while the remainder would board the liner from a couple of Chinook choppers. We would be parachuting from the back of a Hercules C-130 with a one-ton RIB and equipment attached to the backs of our legs, as well as weapons and our 'chutes. On hitting the water, we would have to detach the equipment and then swim like hell to catch the RIB bobbing around in the water.

We arrived at RAF Lyneham in the SBS team vans — ordinary, unmarked vehicles with supercharged engines capable of 120mph with a four-man team inside, as well as all their equipment. We noted that the SAS boys arrived in their fleet of unmarked, special edition Range Rovers, very upmarket, very privileged.

At the briefing in one of the hangars, everything seemed to be fine until the pilot in command of the Hercules casually remarked, 'If, when the RIBs are being deployed, one of them accidentally rips off the tail of the Hercules, it's every man for himself. Just get to any exit as fast as possible and get the hell out of the aircraft. In those circumstances, we will try to keep the plane as stable as possible for as long as possible so that you can all get out. OK?'

The pilot made the statement as if this catastrophic possibility was a normal, everyday occurrence, and we all looked at each other and laughed nervously but we were somewhat taken aback. 'Fuck me,' I thought to myself, 'I knew this exercise was dangerous but not that fucking tough.'

At six o'clock we received final confirmation that the exercise was on and that the QEII would be passing the 'gate position' on time. The 'gate position' was the exact longitude and latitude where we would lie in wait for the liner to arrive before the action began. We all changed into our black water- and fire-repellent overalls and began going through our equipment checks: weapons, signals equipment, parachute. The parachute is then checked by a mate and finally by the Parachute Jump Instructor (PJI) before anyone is permitted to board the Hercules.

As soon as we had all boarded and were ready for take-off, the red emergency lights were switched on and the normal white light turned off. A soft, red light is the best light possible for enhancing one's night vision, for normal white light would cause us all to be 'blind' for more than a minute before our eyesight became fully adjusted to the darkness when we eventually jumped from the Hercules. As we sat and listened to the drone of the engines, nearly all of us fell into a deep sleep. It seems that the noise and the vibration inside these planes is so hypnotic that nearly all parachutists fall into a gentle sleep, despite the fact that within an hour or so we would be leaping into the darkness and parachuting into rough, heavy and freezing waters. The next thing I remember was being shaken awake and suddenly realising where I was. I pulled myself out of my seat and clipped the equipment on to the bottom of my 'chute where it dangled down the back of my legs, making walking almost impossible. When carrying such a weight, all you can do is waddle awkwardly along, looking like a duck. And what makes it difficult to walk is that the gear has to be strapped tightly to your legs otherwise it would be ripped from your body when you leap from the aircraft because of the force of the slipstream.

Because I was coxswain of the RIB, I was first in line waiting to jump. I was sweating buckets because of the gear I was carrying and the water-proof assault overalls we were wearing, which for some unknown reason are called 'frizzies'. I got the 'two minutes' signal from the Jump Instructor and methodically went through my parachute check list one last time. Then the rear doors of the Hercules came down.

'Red on,' the instructor shouted and my heart began to beat faster as the 'ready to jump' light came on.

Seconds later, the green lights flashed on and with a loud clunk the safety pins holding the RIB cradle came off. A welcome rush of lovely cool air wafted in and I was happy to see that the sky was bright with stars, but I had work to do. I reached forward and cracked the two light 'cyalumes' — a chemical mixture which when cracked produces a bright fluorescent glow — on the RIB. I instantly closed my eyes so as not to destroy my night vision.

Then the noise of a terrific 'whoosh' filled the aircraft and the RIB, all one-and-a-half tons of boat, was gone in less than a second. I waddled forward as quickly as I could and threw myself out of the Hercules, immediately throwing my arms out to the side to stop myself spinning around in the slipstream.

'One thousand ... two thousand ... three thousand,' I shouted to myself as I marked the speed of my descent.

'Check canopy,' I shouted out loud and immediately looked up. This is a heart-stopping moment for every parachutist, even if you have jumped 100 or more times. The one terrifying fear that is always present whenever you jump from an aircraft — the dreadful possibility that your 'chute doesn't open. To my relief, as had happened every time I ever jumped from an aircraft, I had a full canopy. Now I could breathe more easily, as my eyes scanned the sea below for the RIB that I knew must be somewhere beneath me.

I would look for a few seconds and then quickly scan the sky around me just in case I was in danger of colliding with one of the other lads who'd jumped with me. Thank God, mid-air collisions in the SBS and the SAS are few and far between, but they are not unknown. I had no wish to become entangled in someone else's 'chute, with the inevitable result of both of us plunging into the sea and then possibly becoming entangled and pulled down beneath the waves. For that, too, can be terrifying, especially in a rough sea.

But I put those thoughts at the back of my mind and concentrated on lining myself up as well as I could before the final run, aiming to hit the water as close to the RIB as possible. I dropped my kit, which fell away although, of course, it was still attached to me with a length of rope. Then I hit the cold, dark water and immediately jettisoned my main 'chute, for if you don't get rid of it quickly there is a danger of being dragged underwater and drowning.

As I surfaced, I realised I was only ten to fifteen metres from the RIB so I put on my fins and swam the short distance on my back, while having a look round to see if I could see anyone nearby. I clambered on to the back of the boat and chucked my kit which was inside my waterproof 'Alison' bag on to the deck. My first job was to take my diver's knife and cut the string holding down the wooden protection panel on top of the boat. Within a minute or so of releasing it, some of the lads had reached the boat and they clambered aboard and started to prepare the equipment for our assault on the liner. A few minutes later, a safety boat came over to us to ask if everyone was OK and then we passed over all the safety equipment we wouldn't need for the exercise. The three other RIBs came powering towards us and we then made contact with the Maritime Patrol Aircraft (MPA), the Nimrod plane guiding us on to the target.

So far, everything was going well and our times were spot-on, an absolute essential in such situations where split-second timing can mean the difference between a successful assault and a bloody cock-up. We were the lead boat, followed by the other SBS team and then the two SAS boats. As coxswain, I was in constant contact with the Nimrod who told me where the QEII was located. The lads sitting in the boat waiting for the action to start were now freezing their bollocks off, as we wear hardly anything under the assault overalls because as soon as you start working, the sweat starts pouring off. So until they swing into action, they just sit and freeze. It's even worse if you have a piss inside the suit.

We were moving along at some speed with our twin engines powering through the water.

Suddenly, the Nimrod navigator came on. 'Whisky 34 Echo. This is Firefly. Target about four miles on a bearing of two-six-zero. Over.'

I could just see the target on the horizon and radioed back, 'Firefly. This is Whisky-three-four-Echo. Target in visual. Awaiting assault order. Out.'

A few seconds later came the order, 'Go, go, go ... I repeat ... go, go, go.'

I floored the throttle and the other three RIBs came into single file behind our boat. It seemed to take us forever to overhaul the QEII — we didn't seem to be getting any closer, despite the fact that we were thumping through the waves. As we approached, I could feel the wash from the ship as she powered along. The closer we came, I looked up to see the immense ship towering above us, gobsmacked by the sheer size of her. As we moved 100 yards behind her, it felt like riding white water rapids and I had to fight like hell to keep the RIB on course while everyone was holding on to the sides for dear life. We were being thrown all over the place with the huge waves being created by the QEII's propellers.

We were now on target and the ladder was 'shot up'. I looked up, realising how tiny our RIB was in comparison with the vastness of the liner. The men in the four boats now had their weapons trained on the upper deck, just in case any terrorists decided to take a look and poked their heads over the stern. If this had been a real attack, the lads would have instantly taken out anyone poking their heads over the stern. We couldn't risk anyone opening fire on us for we would be sitting targets bobbing about on the waves at the stern of the ship.

I then realised that number two RIB had gone AWOL. I couldn't see it anywhere, so I radioed for number three RIB to come up alongside and put its men on to the ladders. But it was proving extraordinarily difficult keeping the RIBs in position near the ship because the wash was throwing us about like corks, despite the strength of our boats and the power of our engines. For a while, it was chaotic as we struggled to keep our boats from smashing into each other. We needed to get all our assault teams up the ladders and on to the ship's decks in the shortest possible time. The assault teams were having tremendous difficulty keeping their feet as they moved towards the ladders with the violent movements of the RIBs over which we had little or no control. Every second counted for it meant that, at this early stage of the assault, we only had a few SBS men aboard and, of course, we had no idea of the terrorists' numbers, weaponry or capability, but we had to plan for the worst-case scenario. Finally, when all my lads had clambered up the ladders, I cut my engines and pulled away, to leave space for number four RIB to take my place and put aboard its SAS team.

Once the upper deck had been secured, I heard over my radio, 'Go, go, go,' the signal for the helicopter assault to swing into action. I looked skyward and out of the darkness I saw the two Lynx helicopters, showing no lights, flying towards us just 50ft above the waves. The Lynx carried snipers who would be used to target any terrorists who had escaped the assault on the ship and were hiding somewhere on one of the top decks. I knew that one of the pilots that day was HRH Prince Andrew, and wondered if he was as nervous as we were on such real-life exercises. I knew he had flown choppers in the Falklands War so he had to have had some guts. A few seconds later, the big Chinook chopper swung into view bringing in the assault teams. The Chinook hovered over the QEII as the teams fast-roped down on to the decks. Then the action really began with muzzle flashes going off in various parts of the liner as our SAS assault teams took on the 'terrorists' who were prepared to keep shooting until exhausting their ammunition. A few hours later, the ship had been re-taken and when the four RIBs had drawn level with the slowing liner, we were offered full run of the ship and a free piss-up in the first-class bar. It was a great way to end an exercise.

When we returned to Poole, the hard work began. Before we were permitted to go on weekend leave, every piece of equipment had to be thoroughly cleaned and made serviceable for the next operation, for the next one could be the real thing. Every weapon, every radio, in fact every piece of equipment that could be cleaned was cleaned and yet we all happily did our bit, because we realised how important that part of the exercise could be. As the debriefing took place with both praise and justified criticism from those judging the exercise, I wondered how different it might be, how much more adrenalin would be needed, had that been a real-life mission with hardened terrorists firing live ammunition. One day I would have that experience, but it would be far from the friendly waters of the English Channel.

CHAPTER SEVEN

I was downing a pint of scrumpy cider in a West Country pub and looking forward to a steak and chips dinner and a glorious weekend with my girlfriend when my pager bleeped.

'Shit,' I said to myself, so that my girlfriend Sarah couldn't hear, 'what the fuck do they want now?'

Because I had hoped this would be a lovely weekend break away from the SBS, I feared the bleep spelt trouble. 'Sod's law,' I muttered to myself.

'Pardon,' said Sarah, 'what did you say?'

'Nothing,' I lied, 'just talking to myself as usual.'

I turned round, casually checked my pager and my eyes nearly popped out of my head.

'Fuck,' I thought to myself and looked again at the pager, checking that I had read it correctly. There were four figures on the pager, not the six figures I had expected. Four figures was the secret code telling us we were needed urgently for an operation; six figures meant we were required to report immediately but only for a training exercise.

What to tell Sarah? All SBS personnel lead secret lives and we are always under orders not to reveal any tasks or missions. Nowadays, more than ever, the SBS work often involves international terrorism or drug-busting missions, which could prove hazardous or even fatal if word got out that the SBS had been called in.

'What's the matter?' I heard Sarah say and she repeated the question a moment later.

'Oh, it's the boss,' I lied, 'it's another of those exercises.'

'What exercises?' she asked. 'You didn't tell me you were going on exercise this weekend.'

'I can't get out of this one,' I said. 'I've got to phone and then I'll know what I've got to do.'

'But I thought we were going to have a lovely

weekend together,' Sarah said, in a voice full of anticipation, which I knew promised gut-wrenching sex.

'Fuck!' I thought as I jumped up and walked over to the phone in the corner. I rang headquarters and spoke to the ops room.

'M Squadron,' I said, when the duty telephonist at Poole answered the phone.

'Sergeant-Major here,' came the voice, 'who's that?'

I gave him my rank and number though I knew him well.

'You have to be back at Poole within four hours from now, and be ready in full-scale equipment. There will be a full briefing in the "ready" room at 2200 hours. OK?'

'Got it,' I replied.

'And don't be late,' he added.

'I won't,' I replied. 'See you later.'

I walked quickly back to Sarah. 'I've got to go.'

'Where?' she asked.

'I've no idea,' I replied, 'probably some drill. But I've got to report to HQ.'

'When?' she asked.

'Even now I'm late,' I said. 'Can I give you a lift back to the flat? I have to leave right now.'

'Really?' she said, unable to understand that any drill exercise could be that urgent.

''Fraid so,' I said, 'no option.'

Sarah looked somewhat peeved but she understood. She knew that I was in the SBS and she also understood that we did sometimes get involved in highly secret missions.

'You can't tell me anything, can you?' she asked.

'No,' I said, 'you know I can't.'

'I know,' she said.

So we went to the car — my grandad's old banger, the Opel Kadett — and I drove Sarah home. Five minutes after walking through the door, I had collected all my gear, kissed Sarah goodbye and was away.

I felt guilty leaving Sarah as I drove flat out, making my way down motorways and across country to Poole. I had only once been stopped by the police when under orders to return urgently to base. On that occasion, I had produced my ID, told the police I was needed in a hurry and they waved me on my way, telling me to go carefully. We had no understanding that we would not be prosecuted in such circumstances, but the traffic cops knew that the SBS were frequently engaged in top-secret operations — when minutes sometimes mattered — and had sometimes turned a blind eye to speeding offences. The police knew that no SBS man would use the excuse frivolously because we are trained to be responsible. And no SBS man would want scorn poured on him by his mates if he was found to be lying to police. We knew that all the police had to do was phone Poole, speak to the Squadron Commanding Officer and find out if we were responding to an urgent call at the time the offence was committed. If we had been found to be simply out joy-riding at the time we would, quite rightly, have had the book thrown at us.

On this occasion, however, luck was with me and though the old Opel Kadett sped along at over 70mph, I never once saw a police car.

I arrived two hours later and the Sergeant-Major told me to get all my kit ready, including two RIBs, and report to the Haslar building for a ten o'clock briefing. The building was dedicated to the legendary Lt-Col HG 'Blondie' Haslar OBE, DSO, Croix de Guerre, a Marine officer who had led the way during World War II with his innovative use of small, fast craft to attack enemy shipping. Haslar was to work closely with Earl Mountbatten in the Combined Operations Development Centre, studying ways in which

British raiders could destroy enemy boom defences, beach obstacles and dock installations, sometimes dropping surface craft from airplanes. Haslar was also one of those responsible for introducing the famous Cockleshell canoes.

Now I had spoken to the Sergeant-Major, I knew that this mission was really on and I could feel the adrenalin building inside me. I ran from his office to my room, stuffed my wash bag and a couple of tracksuits and trainers into my kit bag. I told myself to 'slow down' as I checked all the important gear — webbing, assault kit, radios and tracking devices, before dashing off to the armoury. There I picked up my Heckler & Koch MP5 and my Sig 226, 9mm automatic pistol. I knew I would collect the ammo some time later.

As I walked into the briefing room, everyone was there chattering and whispering, asking if anyone knew what was going on. No one knew a thing.

As the OC walked into the room, there was total silence.

'Right, lads,' he began, speaking in a relaxed manner. 'Customs has requested our help in an off-shore drugs operation. From what we know at this time there is a target vessel, about 50m in length, suspected of carrying three tonnes of cannabis. We don't yet know the exact location of the target, nor the time we will hit it. But from this moment no one is permitted to leave this building. You are all on immediate stand-by to move.'

We all looked at each other realising full well that three tonnes of cannabis represented millions of pounds of someone's money, and that the crew on board the vessel might decide to make a stand against a raiding party. As we chatted among ourselves, the OC was deep in conversation with the Operations Officer and the Customs contact officer.

Two hours later, as we sat around in anticipation, we were given an intelligence up-date. The news wasn't good. We weren't told from where the vessel had sailed, nor where it was due to dock. But we were told that an international crew was on board, a number of them with previous form for drugs trafficking and violent crimes.

'I suggest you get some kip,' we were told. 'At this time, we have no precise times for movement to the target. We'll let you know as soon as possible. In the meantime, the same rules apply; no one is permitted to leave this building.'

I nodded and everyone decided to try to grab

some shut-eye before the action. I dozed off listening to my Walkman. I awoke with a start some time later. It was morning. I must have gone out like a light. Everyone was waking slowly, crawling out of their bags and getting themselves together, shaving and showering. Breakfast followed but still there was no further news. That day dragged on so slowly. We checked our kit, then checked it again and then again. We had started to believe that nothing would happen, that it had all been a waste of time.

Shortly after seven that evening, the OC walked back in. 'I have some news. The operation is to go ahead. We want everyone and all the kit loaded into the team vans and ready to go three hours from now. I shall be handing out route cards to the three drivers but shortly after leaving camp we will be given a police escort to our destination. You all know what you've got to do; we've done it often enough in training. But remember lads, this is a live one.'

We all helped loading the vans and strapping the RIBs on to the specially built Mercedes trucks. Because there was no mad rush to reach our destination, there were no blue lights flashing on the police cars as we drove in convoy and at a steady pace through the night. This was the way the SBS preferred to go into action, quietly and discreetly, causing no alarm, no fuss and without any attention-grabbing behaviour.

Some of the lads dozed, but most of us stayed awake wondering what the operation would entail. Now we were on our way and we knew that there was a real live mission ahead, so the adrenalin was pumping. There was nothing like the thrill, the anticipation of an operation to make all our hard work and training worthwhile. This was the reason we went through hell during training so that, when the moment to strike came, we were able to cope with virtually any eventuality. Sometimes, for months on end, we would go from training exercise to training exercise, but live missions only came once or twice a year.

At Portsmouth we transferred all the gear to HMS Nottingham, a Class 22 frigate, and headed out to sea early on the Monday morning. The Nottingham crew had been told that this was purely a training exercise, but they were expected to work the ship as though this was a major operation. It was expected that we would hit the target ship some 48 hours later and we spent the first day carrying out preparatory drills.

We knew the target ship was being tracked by an RAF Nimrod Maritime Patrol Aircraft, and we had two Lynx helicopters on board which would be used by the snipers in case the target ship decided to strike back at us. During that day of rehearsals, the choppers would take off with snipers on board and practise flying level and sometimes just feet above the sea. They also practised taking off and landing at night with no lights. We all knew that could well be a possibility, which is an awesomely difficult task in combat conditions and in pitch darkness.

For our part, we practised launching and recovering the RIBs so that every member of the two crews knew exactly what he was doing down to the last detail. The second day was spent preparing and checking the equipment, with special emphasis on the guns. We were shown aerial photographs of the target ship and studied pictures of the vessel so that we had a good idea not only of where we could target our assault but, more important, working out the best way of securing the ship after we had boarded. We knew this crew could be armed and were definitely dangerous and we had to assume that they would probably make a fight of it.

After the hectic activity and the concentration on vital details of the mission, time began to drag as we waited for the operation to get under way. We enjoyed a couple of good meals, some of us read paperbacks, others chatted about nothing in particular. We were all on edge, our nerves taut and expectant, waiting for the off. Most of the time I just lounged around while others paced up and down. Some managed to get a few hours shut-eye. The hours ticked by and nothing happened. We were all feeling pissed off and some suggested that the target ship might somehow have managed to escape the net. Eventually, we decided nothing would happen so we turned in and after tossing and turning for a couple of hours, I eventually managed to drift off to sleep.

I awoke with a start. Some of the lads in that cramped cabin were already up and about while others were clambering out of their bunks. Fearful that I might be late, I sat up quickly and banged my head on the bunk above. It was a real crack. 'Shit!' I said and a couple of the lads who had seen what happened cracked a couple of jokes at my expense, but I was too busy trying to get my shit together to worry. It was chaos with everyone moving around at the same time looking for their clothes and equipment, getting in each other's way and swearing like bloody troopers. Someone had kicked my boots under a bunk, so I found myself on my hands and knees scrambling about under the bunks while people were falling over my legs. For the next ten minutes everyone seemed to be swearing, 'fucking' this and 'fucking' that, as they desperately sought to get their gear together. Suddenly, everyone saw the funny side of the situation as we clambered and fell over each other in our enthusiasm to start the operation, and the swearing turned to laughter.

We ran up on deck and began an equipment check. Only then did I look at my watch. It was 6.15am and the sun was just starting to rise over the horizon. I shook my head, wondering what the hell was going on.

'We're not going in broad daylight, are we?' I asked a mate next to me.

'Fucking looks like it,' he replied.

'But we never assault a ship in daylight; we'll be sitting ducks. I can't believe it,' I replied.

'Perhaps they're just checking everything out, readying us for an assault later tonight,' he volunteered.

'Well, why the hell get us out of bed at six in

the morning?' I said, sounding pissed off.

Three hours later on a beautiful May morning, we launched the two RIBs with two teams of four men on each RIB. I was sitting immediately behind the driver with the communications tracking device and an MP5 to cover the first lads to clamber aboard the target ship. It was to be a simultaneous assault with two Lynx choppers and two RIBs hitting the target at the same time.

The helicopters took off with snipers on board, and took up a holding position out of sight of the target ship. They, too, were awaiting the order to 'go'.

I was in almost constant contact with the radio officer on board the Nimrod, who told me where the target ship was located. He gave me a heading and we altered course accordingly. We were tootling along at a few knots an hour on a flat, calm sea under a cloudless, blue sky. The sun was warm but not hot. For a pleasure ride at sea the weather was perfect; for the job we had in hand, it was a complete bastard! We knew the target ship would be so easy to pick out miles away which, of course, meant that those on board the ship would also see us miles away. 'Fore-warned is fore-armed,' I thought to myself and I gripped my MP5 a little tighter and checked the magazines were in place.

Fifteen minutes later, the Nimrod told me we were now nearing the target. We changed course slightly to make sure we approached the ship from astern, hopefully keeping out of sight until the last moment. I tensed with nervous anticipation for within a few minutes we knew we would see the ship and be given the order to attack. I could feel my heart beating, knowing that action was only minutes away. I glanced around me and saw the looks of concern on my mates' faces. No one was smiling. We nodded to each other, pulled the black balaclavas over our faces, cocked our weapons, checked the safety catches and waited for orders.

I felt a tap on my shoulder. Tom, who was sitting directly behind me, pointed to the horizon one or two degrees off our heading. We checked with the Nimrod high above us and they confirmed that there were no other vessels but the target ship in the immediate vicinity. As we continued to advance at a reasonable pace, we could see the silhouette of the target ship, then the superstructure. We had seen so many photographs of the ship we were certain this was the correct target. I felt my hand tighten again around the MP5.

We were now within a few hundred yards of the ship and it was obvious that this mission would now go ahead. There seemed no possibility of aborting. I waited and the ship began to loom larger and larger before our eyes.

'Stand by.'

I knew then that it was only a matter of minutes, maybe seconds.

'Go ... go ... go,' came the command over the radio.

Dave floored the throttles on the massive outboards and the RIB took off. Within seconds our speed increased dramatically. I looked behind to check the other RIB and it, too, had taken off and was hairing along in our wake. We were travelling through the water at about 65 miles an hour, the wind tearing at our clothing. The feeling of excitement, anticipation and exhilaration was fantastic. This was the real thing. If we fucked up we could pay with our lives. We all knew that we could depend on each other, there were no weak links. I felt confident that whatever shit the crew threw at us, we would be able to cope. We would end up in command of that ship whatever happened. If we needed to take out any fuckers who stood in our way, then we would.

As we closed on the vessel, I was convinced that we would be spotted. It was now ten in the morning and the whole bloody crew would be wide awake and going about their duties. I knew there must be at least one and probably two on the bridge, checking for any ships. There was no way that we wouldn't be spotted soon, even though we were homing in on them from astern. I screwed up my eyes, scanning the ship to see if anyone had noticed us, checking for any movement on deck and wondering if, at that distance of a few hundred yards, I would be able to see if they began firing. The wind didn't help, making it bloody difficult to see detail on the ship's deck. From my position it appeared that the crew must have abandoned ship, because I could see no movement whatsoever on board. In reality, I knew that was bollocks but I couldn't bloody see anyone.

As I was straining to see what, if anything, was going on, I heard a tremendous whoosh overhead and instinctively ducked my head and hunched my shoulders. Then I looked up and saw the chopper only a few feet above our heads. From the RIB, the chopper seemed massive and the noise from its whirring engines was deafening. I quickly looked at the vessel now looming large in front of us, convinced that the chopper must have alerted everyone on board.

I saw the Lynx slow above the ship and start to hover as our SBS mates on board threw down the ropes and began to fast-rope on to the deck. But the time for action had arrived. We were travelling at such speed we all but crashed into the side of the vessel. As the RIB rose and plunged by the side of the ship, I kept my MP5 trained on the ship's bridge. But this was very difficult because our lads were now clambering up the ropes to board the vessel and they kept flitting across my line of fire as they made their way on board.

I saw not a soul on the bridge and I heard no firing. But that didn't mean the crew had given in without a fight because the clattering of the chopper blades drowned out all other sounds. We kept the RIB alongside the ship and I continued to aim my MP5 on the bridge. It seemed only a matter of a minute or so, however, when one of the lads put his thumb in the air, signalling that all had gone well. They had secured the ship. Not a shot had been fired.

My mates went through the ship, checking

every cabin, every nook and cranny, making sure no crew members had gone into hiding in a bid to escape arrest. After all the officers and crew had been accounted for, a Lynx helicopter from HMS Nottingham flew the Customs officers to the ship to check the cargo. Their information proved accurate. They found three tonnes of cannabis, one of the biggest hauls ever discovered on a ship heading for Britain.

The Customs officers officially charged and arrested the Captain, officers and crew, who were winched up to the choppers and flown to the Nottingham. A pilot and crew had been brought in to take over the ship and take it into port with a couple of Customs men who remained aboard. We took the RIBs back to Nottingham and hauled them aboard. Two days later, we docked at Portsmouth.

Before steaming into Portsmouth, however, the RIBs and the choppers were taken off the deck of the Nottingham and moved ashore, just in case the media had got wind of the mission and were on the dockside waiting to take pictures of the so-called 'conquering heroes'. The Special Boat Service doesn't work like that. We don't encourage heroes, though many SBS men certainly qualify for the accolade. The SBS are usually involved in operations which are surrounded by secrecy and which are often politically sensitive. Their specialist skills, which are unique to the SBS, means they sometimes use equipment and adopt tactical procedures which are classified, far more so than their counterparts in the more illustrious SAS. Secrecy has always been paramount within the SBS, and the tradition continues to this day.

After a complete debrief and a close examination of how the mission had gone and how we had performed, Customs came in to explain the details of the operation and give us the latest news. They estimated that the three tonnes of cannabis found on board was worth approximately £10.5 million at street value. Five people had been arrested. When the first SBS men hit the deck, all but one of the crew had been sleeping in their cabins totally unaware of any raiders. The only guy on duty, keeping watch on the bridge, had been reading a book. He had seen and heard nothing until he realised that choppers were hovering over the ship and men in black, their faces covered with black balaclavas, were fast-roping down to the deck with their guns at the ready. Wisely, he had decided to take no action.

There were other drugs operations that we took part in off the coast of Britain during the 1990s, although the general public had little or no idea that the Special Boat Service had been responsible for most of the successful interceptions and arrests. The press usually attributed such dare-devil attacks to the SAS, but that never worried us. We much preferred to keep a low profile and let our operations take the credit so that we could remain in the background.

We were on an anti-terrorist exercise in Essex in mid-1995 when we were informed that a job had suddenly come up and that we had to report ASAP to a secret location, a stone's throw from our headquarters in Poole. The first we heard of the operation was while we were sitting in the canteen enjoying a cup of tea.

'Quiet everyone,' said the OC as he walked into the room. 'There's something come up. It's a rush job; a drugs bust somewhere off the south coast. A police escort is on its way here at this very moment and we need to be out of here and on the road as quickly as possible. A full briefing will be given later, but now the most important thing is to get moving. OK? Then let's go.'

That short, snappy call to action sent a thrill

through my body and I wondered what would happen. We ran over to the armoury and picked up all our weapons. Whenever we left Poole to go on exercises, we always took with us a complete kit because we never knew where or when we would be needed. It was assumed that most of the operations would call for immediate action, when minutes were vital, and we needed to have everything with us so we could be on the road within an hour, ready for action.

Not only did we keep our personal weapons in the armoury, but everything else as well, including explosives, entry charges, linear cutting gear and ammunition. As always, we stored our weapons in one van, our ammunition in the second and the explosives in a third. We always travelled in convoy like this for safety reasons. We clambered into a fourth van and set off. Police cars and out-riders, with sirens blaring and blue lights flashing, took up positions ahead and behind the convoy. We sped through red traffic lights, the wrong way round roundabouts and the Dartmouth tunnel had been closed so that we could swoop through at high speed. They didn't want to risk us being held in some traffic jam half-way into the tunnel. Most of the time, we sped along at about 90mph in the specially adapted Ford Transit vans, equipped with 2.9 litre V6 fuel-injection engines churning out 165 brake horse power.

It was great racing along at such speed knowing that we were breaking the speed limit every mile of the way — and with the police urging us on to go faster. But we did have one serious scare. Paul was driving flat out at the time when a car pulled out unexpectedly, a few seconds after the police vehicles had flashed past. Without giving any signal or warning, the car edged out into the centre of the road. Paul took immediate action, swerving to avoid the car that was only travelling slowly. But he could not react quickly enough and we clipped the side of the vehicle. We drove on, followed by the other three team vans. We looked back to see the driver shaking his fist at us, grimacing angrily. We didn't stop nor did we even contemplate stopping. I have no idea what damage we did to the car but, thankfully, we never heard anything about the smash.

As we drove down the M3, it was decided to launch the raid on the unknown vessel from our Poole headquarters. On arrival, we learned that this mission was a major drug bust but that no helicopters would be used, only three RIBs. This was going to be fun.

It took two hours of dedicated, hard work to prepare the three RIBs for the mission. In addition to SBS personnel, each RIB carried SO19 police officers. The officers would be the first to jump from the boat, to lead the assault and make the arrests. It was intended that we would be on hand as back-up, but fully armed and in our traditional all-black SBS kit with balaclavas and, of course, our handguns. The SBS officers had argued with the police that it would be better to let the SBS go in first, capture the drug-runners and then call in the police units. The police decided, however, that this drug bust was their responsibility and they wanted to make the arrests, keeping the SBS as back-up if trouble arose.

We looked at each other and winked. We knew the police officers fancied making the initial arrests to enable them to take the glory. We weren't worried because we prefered to play the background role, stealthily going about our business with ruthless efficiency, without anyone realising that the SBS had been involved.

With everything packed and ready to go, the CO walked in to give us a full briefing.

'We know that the drugs gang we are going

after tonight is a serious, international group of men who have been involved in drug smuggling over a number of years. They are not only involved in drugs but they are also wanted for other serious crimes committed across Europe.'

Then we were briefed by an army lawyer. His words of wisdom, which we were given before every single mission, warned us of the legal problems we could face if we became involved in a gun battle.

'If you get involved in a gunfight and people get injured or killed, then on no account must anyone say a word until I get to the scene. Answer no questions whatsoever; no matter if you are being questioned by Army or Navy officers or even high-ranking police officers. It is vital for what might follow those shootings that you say nothing until I have debriefed you in full. OK?'

We all nodded. We knew the score. In effect, the army lawyer was telling us to 'trust no one'.

At 2200 hours, we made our way down to the RIBs, along with our police officers who were all dressed as we were. There was one important difference, however. They insisted on wearing extensive body armour, which was very effective in stopping high-velocity rounds but totally useless in practice because the armour was so heavy and cumbersome, making movements slow and ponderous. On such missions, we only ever wore light body armour because we were then able to move around at speed, climb ropes fast and, if necessary, tackle a gunman using unarmed combat skills. With full body armour we wouldn't have been able to carry out any of these skills with any speed whatsoever, thus putting our lives at risk.

Having carried out one further check, we were assembled waiting for the order to go. For two more hours, we gently floated around, the engines idling, waiting for the 'off'. It was a cold February night and, despite the thermals we were wearing, we all began to feel the chill wind insinuating our bones. The swear words became more frequent as everyone grew increasingly pissed off with every passing minute. We kept checking our watches, which seemed to be ticking at a snail's pace. Some of us cracked open our flasks and I took a few gulps from mine, which contained hot, strong, black coffee with lots of sugar to help keep up the levels.

There was one good point in our favour. The long wait enabled some of the lads who had considered joining the police force to talk with the two officers, asking their opinions, finding out the attractions and the down side of life as a police officer. But even that conversation eventually dried up and we were left to clock-watch once more. For three more hours we continued bobbing around Poole Harbour, the engines still ticking over quietly, gurgling away in the black water. By 0400 hours we had come to the conclusion that this had been another boring, wasted night and we expected to be 'stood down' at any moment.

I had all but lost interest when over the 'net' came the news that the target vessel had been picked up by radar and was on its way along the English Channel towards us. The boss gave us 15 minutes to collect our shit and get everything ready once more. For one final time we checked our weapons and ammunition, our communications equipment and personal belongings. But this time we had to be ready for instant action.

We knew that, high above the clouds, a Nimrod reconnaissance aircraft had detected the target vessel and that, eventually, we would be guided to its location. Then we would take over for the final, flat-out push to the ship and the assault.

We were given a heading to follow and then, minutes later, the warning order came through. We were within seconds of taking off. We pulled on our balaclavas and cocked our weapons. We were ready. The intention was to circle the target ship slowly and silently at some distance, and then approach it, hoping that the crew and any look-out wouldn't notice us until it was too late. We set off.

Suddenly, the whole fucking area was flooded with brilliant light, as the four RIBs were caught in the full glare of a helicopter's powerful spotlight. We had been lit up like a fucking Christmas tree, exposed to everyone on the target ship who happened to switch their attention to a helicopter suspiciously hovering around at some ungodly hour looking for goodness knows what! We believed in that instant that Customs officers in the chopper above had unwittingly given the game away and exposed us. It transpired that the stupid Customs men on board the Sea King believed they were helping us because they had 'lost' the target vessel and had decided to switch on the spotlight to find it. They hadn't focused on the poor SBS blokes below who were risking their necks putting a raiding party on board a ship that was under the command of dangerous and armed drug smugglers.

Unbelievably, the Customs men had been unaware that we had already located the vessel, knew precisely the course it was sailing, and were positioning ourselves to make the attack. It was obvious that no one had fully appreciated that such an action might alert the crew we were trying to catch off-guard. Such actions gave the drug-runners the option of making a run for it or simply dumping the drugs overboard and pleading innocent. We would have been able to prove nothing without the evidence. The curses poured from our mouths.

Jokingly, one of the lads shouted up to the chopper, 'Why didn't you just phone the fuckers first and tell them we were on our way?' We all laughed, but it had been a serious error which could have put SBS lives at risk.

The boss got on to the 'net' and radioed Poole headquarters telling them what had happened and emphasising that the Customs men aboard the chopper had put the entire mission at risk. A message was immediately flashed from Poole to the chopper telling them to shut off the light and piss off out of the area until called for. Seconds later, the spotlight was doused and the chopper flew away. We waited around for a few minutes, expecting the job to be called off and waiting for orders to return to base as the mission had been seriously compromised. But no.

Thirty minutes later, still awaiting orders, the 'net' opened up.

'Target vessel has been lost to radar but understood it could be near your position.'

We asked what type of vessel we were searching for.

'It's an RIB like yours but exact size or power unknown.'

I shut off the engine until it was barely idling and we all strained our ears trying to pick up the sound of another RIB powering away not far from our location. Our three RIBs scattered, trying to cover as great an area as possible, as we searched for the target boat. I could see the other RIBs bobbing gently about, sailing along at only a few knots, searching for the missing boat. But within a few minutes I even lost sight of our black-and-grey RIBs because they blended in so well with the shore as a background.

Suddenly, a voice came over the 'net'. 'Look over by the yacht club. Lights. They look like tail lights of a vehicle parked near the sea. That could be our men.'

I grabbed the night-sights and peered into the darkness. Suddenly I caught them. It was the back of a 4x4 Land Rover or something similar. It seemed to be manoeuvring to get a boat out of the water.

That was all the evidence the boss wanted. 'Go, go, go,' he shouted, 'I repeat go, go, go.'

I nailed the throttle and we took off towards the yacht club, weaving in and out of the yachts and boats moored haphazardly in the bay, swerving all over the place, missing some of them by inches as I tried to maintain our top speed and keep the bloody RIB upright. The last thing I wanted to do was over-stew it and end up in the bloody water. I was concentrating hard, straining every muscle to keep the RIB going at a flat-out rate of knots. The lads were sitting in their positions, their hands gripping the grab handles for dear life, their feet under straps on the bottom preventing them being bounced around too much. Riding an RIB at that speed and throwing it around every few yards knocks the hell out of everyone on board. It's no picnic but hard, fucking work simply trying to sit still, riding the horrendous bumps and jolts as the boat crashes through the waves. Some SBS guys end up with serious back injuries riding the RIBs at speed.

Within ten minutes or so, all three RIBs were inside the marina and we could clearly see a group of men desperately trying to pull a boat out of the water and attach it to the back of a 4x4 vehicle.

There was only one way to capture this lot and that was to drive the RIB on to the beach, leap out and arrest the men who were surrounding the vehicle and boat. I slammed the RIB into neutral and the boat instantly slowed. We must have been travelling at around 20mph when we hit the beach, and the RIB came to an abrupt halt in the soft sand.

As ordered, the two police officers were the first out of our boat, leaping on to the sand. But the gear they were carrying, including their personal weapons, and the heavy body armour proved too much for them. As they landed, they simply fell head-first into the sand. That was the end of their parlour game, their glory days were over. The lads jumped from the boat and used the backs of the fallen coppers as a springboard to leap on to the sand. As each SBS guy leapt from the boat on to the backs of the coppers, they pushed the police officers deeper into the sand, ignoring their cries for help. There was no time to stop and help them. As far as we were concerned these smugglers in front of us may have been armed and dangerous.

Our only thought was to arrest them, grab their weapons and secure any drugs that might be on the boat or in the 4x4. The cops could take care of themselves.

'Lie down, get down,' we shouted at the bunch of men who turned to face us. The men seemed too shocked to move. They simply stared at us, their mouths open, a look of fear in their eyes as 18 men all dressed in black overalls with machine pistols in their hands came racing towards them.

We screamed at them, 'Get on the fucking floor now … lie face down … don't fuckin' move … stay still or you're dead.'

At one time there were maybe five or six of us shouting and swearing at the men, deliberately shocking them, making them feel nervous and vulnerable. Other SBS men ran into the buildings and outhouses, searching for other accomplices, checking out the area in case there were others in hiding. At all times we had to presume that some men on that mission would be armed. What we didn't know was whether they would be stupid enough to use their weapons on us. If they had done so we would have taken them out without a second thought.

One man stood stock still looking at us, not moving a muscle, paying no heed to our orders, so someone went up to him and gave him a right cross, knocking him senseless. He crumpled to the ground and didn't move, so someone kicked him, yelling at him to lie on his face and keep still. Another man looked up to see what was going on, so he received a good, hard kick on the side of the head and was told to lie face down. Not surprisingly, he obeyed. As one SBS man went to put plasti-cuffs around a suspect's hands and feet, another man began to sit up. As if from nowhere, an SBS man sent him flying, catching him under the chin with the full force of his boot.

'When I tell you to lie down, I mean LIE DOWN,' he screamed at him. 'If you move another muscle you'll be a dead man.' And he placed the barrel of his Heckler & Koch on the man's neck, pushing his face into the ground.

'Stay like that,' yelled the SBS man. 'Don't move a fucking muscle,' he warned as the plasti-cuffs were placed tightly on the man's wrists and ankles.

One by one, we went around the six men, holding the barrel of the machine pistol to the backs of their necks as we asked each of them in turn, 'Are you carrying a gun? Is anyone carrying a gun?'

When no one answered, we shouted louder, telling them to yell their answers aloud if they didn't want a bullet in the back of the neck.

'No guns, no guns,' they all shouted, their voices quivering with fear.

While half-a-dozen of us stayed with the prisoners, others checked the boats on the marina, the yacht club, the beach huts, everywhere someone could possibly be hiding or where the prisoners may have stashed their drugs. We found nothing. We searched the 4x4, a Mitsubishi Shogun, as well as the 22ft-long rigid inflatable which had a 150hp Yamaha motor capable of moving in excess of 50mph. Nothing was found.

Within five minutes of our arrival on the marina, about 30 police cars came screaming at speed into the yacht club car park and dozens of officers came running across to where we were standing, our guns still pointing towards the men on the ground lying motionless at our feet.

When the senior officers asked who was in charge, we pointed to the hapless cops who had by now managed to climb to their feet and stagger to the marina where we were standing. Their gear was covered in sand and sea water and they didn't look very happy bunnies. One or two also gave us filthy looks, but they didn't say anything.

Over the following few days, police divers searched the Solent and eventually discovered two tons of cannabis, packed in hessian and wrapped in plastic that the crew must have thrown overboard when they saw the chopper's spotlight searching the sea earlier. As a result of that hit, 13 people from various parts of the country were arrested and tried at the Old Bailey. They were all found not guilty.

There were perhaps three or four major drugs busts every year in which the SBS were called in to take part. Drugs busting became one of our favourite activities because we never knew what reception we would receive whenever we raided a vessel. We were always prepared for the worst — a serious fire-fight — but thankfully that hardly ever occurred. On most occasions we received very little opposition from any of the crews ferrying the illicit drugs, but SBS senior officers believed the principal reason for that was the manner in which we had been trained to carry out such raids.

Speed, determination, surprise and ruthless handling of the drug smugglers were designed to knock the stuffing out of those guarding the drugs, so that the thought of having a go at us never entered their minds. And we did play it tough in those situations. We knew that major drug smuggling schemes, involving the movement of large quantities of drugs into Britain by sea, were carried out by unscrupulous international gangs who carried guns and were prepared to use them if and when necessary.

Whenever we raided a ship, boat or yacht suspected of carrying large quantities of drugs, we hit them hard. We always carried guns, usually machine pistols, on those raids and we had to be prepared to use them if necessary. But we never fired unless we were fired on. If any smugglers had been stupid enough to start a fire-fight, we would have used every means possible to ensure our safety and make arrests. If that meant shooting and killing some of them, then that was the penalty they risked for resisting arrest using arms.

In the autumn of 1995, we were given the luxury of a week's notice to prepare to raid a suspected drugs vessel. But there was one major problem. HM Customs had information concerning a yacht which they believed was heading for the north-east coast of Britain and, it was understood, that the yacht would meet some other local vessel to take the goods and ferry them to a discreet location for distribution. Our job was to hit the yacht before any drugs were handed over, hoping to catch both crews.

Some days later, we were told that there was every possibility that the yacht might stay out in the North Sea meaning that the RAF's big CH-47 Chinook helicopters would be needed to pick up our heavy 28ft RIBs and drop them and us into the sea some miles off the coast.

As the day drew closer, we then learned that the yacht was perhaps 60 miles off the Northumbrian coast, which meant that the Chinooks would only have sufficient fuel to stay around the area for a matter of minutes before dropping the RIBs and the two teams of Black Troop. Even with extra fuel pods, the Chinook would be virtually out of its safety range.

We took off in high spirits, despite the weather and sea report which forecast a gale force eight wind, severe rain storms and a sea state number seven. This was going to be one hell of an operation working in such atrocious conditions. As we sat waiting for the 'off', we looked at each other with half-smiles on our lips. There was no need to say anything; we all knew we were going to be operating in deep shit.

To heighten our anxiety as we headed out into the North Sea, unable to see anything in the blinding rain, which made the chopper's wipers all but useless, we heard from the Nimrod maritime patrol aircraft high above us that they were having problems locating the bloody yacht. Sixty miles out into the North Sea and we were in deep trouble. The pilot told us that he was already operating at emergency levels of fuel with the indicator in the red danger zone. We had to decide whether to go ahead with the mission or abort it. And this decision had to be made with the Nimrod crew reporting that they had not yet located the yacht!

Almost at that second, the Nimrod came up reporting that the 40ft yacht had been located and we were about 20 miles behind it.

'OK, let's go,' the boss said.

'Fuck,' I thought, 'this is going to be no picnic.'

I caught the eye of one or two of my mates and it was obvious we were all having the same thoughts: 'This is going to be one hell of a mission.'

The RIBs were gently lowered by the

Chinook until they were about ten feet above the sea swell. Then we fast-roped down into the RIBs. When we were all sitting in them the thumbs-up sign was given to the chopper crew man and the RIBs were lowered into the water. Seconds later, the slings were cut away and we were on our own, the rain lashing our faces, the gale tearing at our clothes and the waves running at some 25 – 35ft.

We checked our bearings and took off after the yacht with the waves crashing over the front of the RIBs, drenching us in seconds and filling the boat. We stared out into the night and could hardly see more than a few feet in front of us. And the target yacht already had a 20-mile start on us. The RIBs each had a 150-mile range but we had no idea at what speed the yacht was travelling. We had to power on and, despite the high seas, we were fairly ripping along at around 25 knots. Some of the lads were vomiting their guts up as we bounced along and our bodies were taking a real hammering every time the RIB hit a wave, smashing us down on our spines as we clung for dear life on to the grab handles in front of us.

'I volunteered for this,' I thought to myself, cursing at the weather and the sea as we crashed our way through the waves in truly frightening conditions. At any moment, I felt we could lose someone overboard, despite the fact that everyone was strong, fit and highly trained. But none of us had ever been in action in such atrocious conditions. And we had certainly never trained in such a sea.

After two of the most gruelling and desperate hours of my entire life, during which one's strength had been sapped to zero, we heard from the Nimrod that we were now only a couple of miles or so from the target yacht. I slowed and reached for my night-vision goggles and could just make out the yacht, but in the dreadful conditions it was difficult to be sure. After further conversation with the Nimrod, it seemed that the yacht I could see was indeed our target.

We continued to gain on the yacht and within 15 minutes or so we had reached striking distance. I gave the thumbs up to the lads, powered towards the target and threw the RIB into neutral. Two of the lads leapt aboard, their machine pistols at the ready, while others secured our RIB to the yacht. I can remember seeing a look of sheer astonishment and fear on the face of the man at the helm, before I heard our lads screaming at him and one other man to lie down and shut up.

Our two lads were yelling at them, telling them not to move, checking to see if they had weapons on board, ordering them to lie face down. The other crew man didn't want to co-operate, so he was smashed in the face and told to lie down. He realised we meant business and finally obeyed. But he began to argue, lifting his head, asking questions. He was given two hefty kicks to the head and stomach and told to lie down and shut up.

The skipper also seemed to be moving. And the lad with the barrel of his Heckler & Koch in the skipper's neck told him to keep still and not to move. Though both the skipper's hands and feet had been plasti-cuffed, he kept moving backwards, so our lad pistol-whipped him across the back of the head half-a-dozen times ordering him to lie still. Finally, he discovered that the skipper was, in fact, being pulled back by the other SBS man on board. He didn't apologise. He just stopped hitting the man.

We searched the yacht's hold and discovered two tonnes of cannabis resin which we were informed later would have been worth about £7,500,000 on the streets. There were no guns on board, so we called up HM Customs and told them that the mission had been successfully completed, and waited for their arrival. An hour later, Customs arrived in a cutter to tow the yacht and its drugs back to harbour. We were then only about five miles off the coast and the seas had subsided somewhat.

The SBS RIBs escorted the cutter and the yacht back to shore. But we realised that the yacht was taking on water and as we headed back to the coast our men on board considered it very unlikely that the yacht would make it. In fact, the yacht suddenly began to fill and the weight of the yacht, half full of water, threatened to break off the back of the cutter which could have caused major problems for the Customs crew on board. Finally, just off Newcastle, the decision was taken to cut the tow line and let the yacht sink. In fact, there was little option, for the yacht would not have made it to the shore.

But the druggies of Northumbria had heard of the sunken yacht and its cargo. As the word spread far and wide, droves of young people began taking walks along the coastline, searching for the manna which they hoped would drift on to the beach on the incoming tides. The police were also there patrolling, but neither they nor the awful weather stopped those keen on getting hold of the shit, returning night after night in search of the illegal drugs. Many were chased off and some were arrested and held, but after a week the druggies and the police called it a day. The two men on the yacht were charged and convicted. But that was one job I had no wish to repeat. It had been hell, but that was the life one expected in the SBS.

CHAPTER EIGHT

Many British soldiers were to be blooded as a result of Saddam Hussein's invasion of Kuwait in 1990, whether they served in Kuwait and Iraq during the Desert Storm offensive or whether, like me, they were involved in the mopping-up exercises in the months following the war. Many US, British and French Special Forces were also brought in to try to protect the Kurds in northern Iraq and the swamp Arabs of southern Iraq from Saddam's ruthless Presidential Guard.

We had first landed just inside Iraq near the Turkish border, where we had been involved in the fire-fight described earlier, when stopping the

Presidential Guard deserters as they fled by car. But my life of luxury, enjoying all the facilities provided by the US Government for their Marines and chopper personnel, had come to an end all too soon and I had been sent off to join 40 Commando, a unit of 400 men who had been ordered to patrol about 65 miles deep inside Iraq. Intelligence had located one of Saddam Hussein's newly built summer palaces at Dahuk in the foothills of the northern mountain range, where Saddam could find respite from the scorching summer sun that turned most of the country into parched desert during the hottest months when daytime temperatures would sometimes reach 140° in the shade!

We were tasked to set up road-blocks and vehicle check-points (VCPs) along the metal road and stop and search all vehicles travelling north, east or west. Not surprisingly, there were no vehicles travelling south towards Baghdad. Intelligence informed us that we would have a busy time because they understood that between 200,000 and 300,000 Kurdish refugees were on the move, fleeing the towns and villages in the centre and south of the country and heading towards the protection of the mountains. They feared Saddam

Hussein would send his troops to attack them in the aftermath of his humiliation at the hands of the American-led force which had so easily routed his Army. We were also expected to protect the Kurdish refugees from any Iraqi attacks. We knew, and many of us secretly hoped, that on this mission we might see some real action.

When we arrived at our planned destination, we set up road-blocks and vehicle check-points and stopped every car as they crawled through the road-block at a snail's pace. The great majority were Kurdish refugees fleeing north, but perhaps one in every ten vehicles was driven by Iraqis, nearly all of whom were carrying arms. We didn't bother to determine if these were army deserters or even if they were members of the infamous Presidential Guard, our orders were simply to cross-question them, confiscate all their weapons and order them to return the way they had just come. Where they went after that we didn't care, as long as they didn't try to head north, towards the Kurdish encampments. Assigned to our Commando unit was a well-educated Iraqi who had been studying in London when the war began and had volunteered to act as an interpreter. It made our job so much easier, as he could explain and, if necessary, argue with those Iraqis posing as Kurds.

After some weeks at the VCP I was assigned to a new patrol of eight men and we were ordered to set up an Observation Post (OP) half-way up a mountain looking down on Saddam Hussein's summer palace a mile or so distant. The palace was a large, two-storey building painted white with a bright red-tiled roof and looked like a vast Spanish-style villa surrounded by a 10ft-high wall. Armed sentries guarded the main gate and patrolled the walls which were about 100ft from the main palace building. Within half-a-mile was a newly constructed air-strip which was linked to the palace by a metal road.

We had recced our OP during a night patrol and over the following two nights, under cover of darkness, we dug our way into the side of the mountain so that all eight of us could take shelter and, hopefully, remain out of sight of the palace guards. We camouflaged the top of the dug-out with chicken wire, covered that with hessian sacks, and then threw sand-coloured earth on top. Armed with binoculars and spy-scopes, and using night-vision sights, we could see exactly what was going on inside the compound. In all, we counted only 16 guards, who obviously worked duty rotas, meaning that only eight were on duty at a time.

For fire-power, we had brought along two light support weapons, which in effect were SA80s with a long barrel and bipod stand, and which used 30-round magazines. We also had six ordinary SA80 rifles and HE grenades. Each man had six magazines plus eight mags for the light support weapon, so we would have been able to stand our ground in a short fire-fight. The hope was that we would never have to use our weapons while keeping an eye on the summer palace, but just keep the place under observation in case of any increased activity which could have heralded the arrival of Saddam Hussein himself, or army commanders planning further attacks on the Kurds.

Our routine never varied. Two men were on watch at a time while the remaining six slept, ate or simply relaxed in the dug-out. By day we were all but trapped in the dug-out because moving during daylight would reveal our position to the Presidential Guard. At night, of course, we would come and go as we pleased, stretching our legs as we exercised behind the mountain, totally out of sight of anyone in the palace compound, even if they did have the benefit of night-vision sights.

After a couple of weeks of tedious boredom, we were woken at about 2.30am by the sound of gunfire. I had been asleep and woke with a start, wondering who was firing at whom, and why.

'What's going on?' someone called softly, wary of how far our voices might travel across the hillside.

'Looks like gunfire inside the palace,' came the reply from the shadow of the Marine at the edge of the OP.

'Who's shooting at whom?' asked someone else.

'Not a fucking clue,' came the reply.

A radio call was made by our wireless operator to HQ reporting the firing inside the palace grounds.

Minutes later, the network opened again. 'Any of our patrols involved in the fire-fight?'

'Negative.'

A minute later came the order, 'Just observe and lie low.'

I felt annoyed and a little cheated. Here we were within a few hundred yards of Saddam's Presidential Guard using their firearms, and we weren't allowed to mount an assault, taking out the guards before going through the palace.

We strained our eyes to try to see what the hell was going on but it was difficult to make out anything. Whenever the guns were fired we could see the flashes from the muzzles of the AK-47s because they always leave a tell-tale flash, unlike our SA80s which hardly emit any flash at all. But it was impossible to tell who was shooting at whom, which made it even more frustrating. We wondered if there had been a ferocious argument inside the palace which had got out of hand, or if there had been a rebellion by some of the occupants or, simply, whether they had been attacked by a rogue Kurdish troop seeking revenge on the hated Presidential Guard.

Then suddenly, as we were lying low and simply observing the fire-fight, one or two rounds hit the rock face around our OP.

'What the fuck was that?' asked someone, though we all knew a round had hit somewhere nearby.

'What the fuck are they up to now?' asked someone.

And another voice in the darkness replied, 'Has anyone any idea what the fuck is going on?'

There was silence, for we were all confused by what had happened. It seemed impossible that the guards had seen us, especially at night, and because of the extraordinary precautions we had taken when setting up the OP. We all waited, listening for incoming fire, and seconds later some more rounds came our way, hitting the rock all around the OP.

'We've been targeted,' someone said.

'Not so sure,' someone else volunteered.

The rounds were coming in about one or two every ten to fifteen seconds, which seemed odd if our dug-out had been spotted and was now being targeted. We would have expected far heavier incoming fire if we had been observed, because we had to presume that the Palace Guard would have been supplied with significantly heavier weapons than simply AK-47s and hand-guns.

As more rounds landed near the OP, we discussed whether we should call for assistance, calling in helicopter gun-ships to attack the gunners in the palace grounds or make a fighting withdrawal from our OP back along the road to base where we could rendezvous (RV) with a chopper to take us out of the area.

Suddenly, the firing escalated and we could hear and see hundreds of rounds being fired by the guards, many of which were coming our way.

They must have simply put their safety catches on automatic and fired a whole magazine each before re-loading, not caring whether they hit their target. Within the space of five minutes, they must have fired 1,000 rounds or more. We had to presume that the guards had ample supplies of ammunition.

The Section-Corporal in command of our patrol decided that we were now under threat, even if we weren't being directly targeted by marksmen. The time had come to show our presence and, hopefully, warn the Presidential Guard to quit firing or risk being attacked. We knew that they would have no idea how many men were on the mountainside but we were fairly sure a patrol of just 16 men would not want to risk a fire-fight with highly-trained commandos.

'Charlie Team, return fire,' came the order and the four of us in Charlie Team moved to the front of the dug-out and began putting down suppressive fire, firing one round every four or five seconds in the hope of making the defenders lie low and stop returning fire. We knew the Guard would have problems picking out our precise position because of the tiny muzzle-flash from our SA80s.

After a few minutes, our Section-Corporal said, 'Charlie Team, stop; Delta Team, carry on.' They crawled up and took over our positions and resumed the suppressive fire. As we strained to look at the effect our fire was having on the defenders, it seemed that the gun-fire in the compound was becoming more sporadic. Now, only the odd round seemed to be coming our way.

About 20 minutes later, our Section-Corporal called 'Cease fire.'

We noticed only a few more isolated muzzle-flashes inside the compound and then silence. Absolute silence. We could see the silhouettes of a few men walking around the palace grounds, but that was all. We radioed headquarters and gave a contact report. We immediately set up our night-vision equipment to see whether we had been compromised during our fire-fight and, more importantly, to check whether the Iraqis had decided to send out a patrol to search for us, their attackers.

We spent the next hour or so scouring the darkness trying to see what the hell was going on and, at the same time, making sure no one was about to come around the mountain and lob a couple of grenades into our OP. Then we heard the rumble of a heavy vehicle and saw a troop carrier roll into the compound and come to a stop. As dawn was breaking, we saw six bodies being carried from the palace to the troop carrier and then it drove away. Later, under cover of darkness, and several hours after the shooting had ceased, we made our way out of the OP and returned to base for debriefing.

Later, we would discover from Intelligence reports that the firing had started when a dozen or so PPK soldiers — the principal Kurdish military wing — had attacked the palace hoping to ransack the place and make off with whatever food, weapons, ammunition and booty they could carry. They had been surprised by the Guard and the four-hour fire-fight had followed, ending with the PPK making a fighting withdrawal under heavy fire, leaving four fatalities behind. They had managed to kill four of the Presidential Guard. It was presumed that they thought the incoming fire from our dug-out on the mountainside had been from other PPK gunmen, but had not dared move out of the Presidential compound to attack them. When our firing stopped, at about the same time as the fire-fight in the compound had ceased, the Guard must have presumed that we, too, had decided to pull back.

Within a couple of weeks of that fighting withdrawal by the Kurdish rebels, it was the turn of 40 Commando, to whom I had become attached, to withdraw from front-line duty. But our withdrawal was unfortunately shameful and embarrassing.

Each day, women would bring their families of young children and babies to see us, to ask for food and whatever clothing we could give them. Without exception, the poor Kurds looked wretched and pathetic and yet there was little we could give them. But the trauma began for me and my mates when the Kurds realised that we were about to leave and return home to the UK.

We knew, and more importantly, the Kurds knew, that Saddam Hussein's ruthless brutal forces were only a mile or so away from our front line. The Kurds knew that within days, if not hours, of our withdrawal, the Iraqi forces would return to vent their anger on the poor Kurdish rebels who had openly sided with the British and American forces. The Kurds had already experienced the despicable tactics of Saddam Hussein when he had killed hundreds of Kurds, including women and children, in chemical attacks on their villages. For two decades, the Kurds in northern Iraq had had to seek shelter from attack in the mountain ranges, for the only weapons at their disposal were AK-47s and a few machine-guns, mortars and hand-grenades. But they, of course, had proved useless against Iraqi air attacks and constant artillery bombardment. And the food in the mountain ranges was sparse and difficult to find and cultivate, and they only had caves in which to hide when the fierce winter cold and snows arrived.

Now we were about to leave them.

The mood over our camp was sombre. I found it difficult, indeed, all but impossible, to look the young mothers in the eye as I gave them all the food I could lay my hands on. I couldn't even look at the little children with whom I had always played and given sweets to and anything else I thought they might like. I knew that we were about to desert them in a most callous, inhuman manner because we all knew that it was very likely they would be dead within days of our departure. Even today, eight years later, I can still see the pleading eyes of the women begging us not to leave them to their fate. And, even worse, I can remember obeying orders telling them through clenched teeth and tears in my eyes that we were not pulling out and deserting them. It gave me a heart-wrenching feeling of guilt. Those are the times that being a soldier is hell. It eats you up inside and makes you wonder why you are prepared to risk your life carrying out some military task only to desert the poor, wretched people you came to rescue, on their own and with no means of protecting themselves against the enemy.

40 Commando were on active patrol along the 37th parallel no-fly zone and we knew that not too far south would be the Iraqi forces and what was left of their armoured regiments. We had been led to believe that there were about 100,000 Kurdish men, women and children in our immediate vicinity who would be at risk whenever the order came to pull out.

We were given 48 hours' notice to withdraw, and during that time we gave as much kit and food as possible to the Kurdish people who had been visiting our camp over the past month or so. I scoured the camp looking for stuff to give them and my mates did the same. Food, of course, was the best gift we could offer, particularly tinned food which would last longer. We gave our watches, all our civilian clothes, socks and T-shirts. To one little lad to whom I had given food most days, I gave my pocket knife, and I can still remember the look of happiness and excitement in his eyes when I told him he could keep it. And I got a severe bollocking when I suggested that we should leave behind one of our clapped-out Land Rovers that was on its last legs. I guessed some Kurdish mechanic would have been able to make good use of it. But I was told that was a 'bloody stupid' idea and to forget it. As a result, orders were issued that no military equipment whatsoever would be left behind.

40 Commando just couldn't move out in broad daylight. We hadn't got the guts or the strength of character to watch the faces of the women, dressed in their colourful, ragged, dirty dresses, whom we knew would plead and weep for us to stay a little longer. And they did weep and plead and their children, caught up in the trauma, began to cry also. They saw what was happening; they knew what we were doing, packing and making ready to depart. We told them we were staying but they couldn't be fooled. They knew for certain, which made our getaway all the more heart-rending for us. So we departed as silently as

possible at the dead of night, under cover of low cloud and darkness, feeling wretched and ashamed. That night I felt anger and bitterness at what we were doing and frustrated that we could do nothing to help them, those people we had come to save and protect. In fact, there could be no denying the fact that we were betraying the Kurdish people, for they had become our allies in the war against Saddam Hussein. We would not forget that those same Kurdish people had been encouraged by Britain and America to rise up and attack the Iraqi forces in the north at the time the UN force was attacking from the south of the country through Kuwait. They had attacked the Iraqis and fought courageously against heavily armed forces. Now we were leaving them to defend themselves against their arch enemy.

We travelled by Land Rover and truck across the desert to Inzilik near the border with Turkey, Iraq and Syria and we were guided to the American base there. It was like something from a Hollywood movie. We were welcomed like long-lost brothers by the American forces who were all spick and span and looked like movie extras on some film set in their clean, crisp, well-pressed uniforms and whiter-than-white T-shirts. We

243 / NOT BY STRENGTH BY GUILE

looked like a bunch of dirty, sweaty, sand-blasted commandos who had just arrived from the front bringing with us our weapons and ammunition.

'Gee, where have you guys bin?' was the greeting from a well-built US Army Sergeant who seemed surprised to find that there had been a war going on just a few hundred miles from where he was standing.

We pointed down the road behind us.

'Don't bother about that,' said the Sergeant, 'just make yourselves at home. Any Limey is welcome here.'

The base was out of this world. Not only were all the barracks smart, clean and comfortable, but there were showers and baths, and a great PX store where you could buy almost anything a man could need. It went without saying that there was a McDonald's and a Burger King to make the lads feel at home. But, astonishingly, for what had been described as a forward base, there was a cinema and an ice-skating rink!

After we had sorted everything out and found places to sleep, we were then told we would be given $33 a day each for food. And the food was not only great, with vast steaks and burgers, but really cheap. Within 24 hours it seemed as though the war and the sweaty, hot conditions we had been forced to endure in the desert had been a century ago. Within a matter of days, however, our holiday camp stay was over and we were ready to fly back to Britain.

That flight wasn't bad either. The Monarch airliner, chartered for our homeward flight, had been well prepared. The aircraft was full of beer and the stewardesses looked as though they had been recruited from the Baywatch TV show. They were gorgeous. Well, to say we got hammered on that trip was an understatement. We drank the plane dry. Before we landed there was not a single alcoholic drink left on the aircraft. We were all in a sorry state and yet, somehow, we managed to behave ourselves, despite the fact that none of us had seen a beautiful English girl for months. They described us as a great bunch of lads who had behaved 'like gentlemen'. We liked that compliment for it didn't happen too often.

Training on board
the *Sir Tristram*.

An RIB drop: the foremost parachute holds the RIB,
the others hold the men!

Top left: One of the SBS team, under a GQ360 square parachute.

Top right and below: Underway training.

In training.

In Iraq, doing pistol practice (*above*) and with my friend (*below*).

Top: With one of the team in Northern Ireland.

Below: On an RIB at Carlingford Lock, Northern Ireland.

Top: A Royal Marine Lynx Helicopter landing in Iraq.

Below: A Kurdish child, holding my gun.

Top: A C-130 stretched Hercules with on-board fuelling attachment.

Below: A swimming delivery vehicle being raised in the South of France.

CHAPTER NINE

Champagne was flowing, the wedding party was in full swing, the band was playing all the favourite songs and 150 guests were drinking and dancing in the marquee set up in the hotel grounds. The midsummer's night air was still warm and humid and couples, the men in morning suits and the women in summer dresses, were walking arm-in-arm through the hotel's beach-side gardens enjoying the warm sea breeze. The young couple who had been married earlier that day were about to say their farewells and set off on their honeymoon.

The guests could hear the drone of a low-flying aircraft, but they paid little heed for this was Studland Bay near Poole in Dorset and local people were quite used to low-flying RAF planes in that area.

But as the RAF C130 cargo jet passed overhead and disappeared out to sea, the guests in the marquee heard a piercing scream. Some ran out to investigate.

Suddenly, from out of the sky, two men dressed entirely in black came crashing down on to the lawn in front of the marquee, their parachutes dragging behind them. Another parachutist landed on the roof of the hotel some 30ft from the ground and slid down the tiles, unable to stop himself crashing to the ground. Fortunately, he landed on top of a table on the lawn which helped to break his fall, otherwise he could have received severe injuries. Falling 30ft is no joke. Another man could be seen hanging from overhead telegraph wires and the wedding guests watched in amazement as he took out a knife and cut the straps before falling 20ft to the ground. Thankfully, he was also uninjured. A number of women screamed and ran into the marquee as several parachutists, looking menacing in their black wet-suits, continued to land on the lawns.

No one had the faintest idea what the hell was going on.

On the road near the hotel, motorists had to take evasive action as two parachutists, also dressed in black wet-suits, suddenly appeared in their headlights as they landed in the middle of the road, their 'chutes dragging across the road and bringing the traffic to a sudden halt. Some motorists were alarmed at what they saw; others leapt from their cars believing the parachutists to have been injured landing on the tarmac but the two men were fine, only apologising for the trouble they had caused as they fought to control their 'chutes during their descent.

Two or three other parachutists landed on the beach, but one poor bastard went straight through the roof of a beach hut. Thank goodness no one was staying there that night, as some people do, for they would have received a very rude awakening. The poor guy who landed on the hut twisted his ankle badly as he hit the roof, but he managed to cut the straps and hobbled on to the hotel lawns in search of medical help. He, for one, binned his 'chute because it was obviously trashed.

Another unfortunate lad landed in a tall tree

and a branch went through his throat. He had to be helped down after we released his 'chute. He was rushed to hospital with part of the branch still in his throat. He needed 30 stitches but was OK. As I struggled to help the guy down from the tree, I was convinced someone must have been killed in that fateful drop.

It was July 1995 and a trials team of the SBS were practising the late-night parachute drop of a heavyweight 28ft-long, 3-ton RIB, the heaviest RIBs ever to be dropped from an aircraft. We had taken off from Boscombe Down in Dorset, one of the RAF's top-secret bases. On board were four civilian scientists and ten SBS parachutists, all part of the trials team examining the practicalities and difficulties of dropping heavyweight RIBs from C130s Hercules aircraft. The RAF crew were all members of Special Forces, the élite flyers.

The plan was to drop the RIB out to sea off the Studland coast and the ten-man SBS team would jump immediately afterwards, swim to the RIB and clamber aboard. But it didn't exactly go according to plan. A sudden wind was responsible for the near-disaster that brought havoc to the young couple's wedding celebrations. The experiment had gone wrong from the very beginning with five false starts that day, when each time the word went out that we were about to board the aircraft a new weather report forecast high winds and the drop had had to be postponed. As dusk settled over Boscombe Down and we prepared to turn in for the night, the meteorological boffins reported a break in the gusting wind and the decision was taken that the experiment should go ahead.

As usual in such situations, everything became a last-minute rush and we were taken out to the aircraft that was waiting on the tarmac in a dilapidated Land Rover that must have been about 20 years old. We picked up our parachutes and checked and re-checked them as usual and someone discovered that they were all out of date. And, as we all knew only too well, no parachute drop should take place with any out-of-date equipment because of the inherent danger.

'Don't worry,' said the Jump Instructor, the man in charge, 'everything will be all right. It's only a training jump from a low height.'

We looked at each other and wondered whether we should accept the instructor's opinion. But we knew he was a very competent, highly professional instructor and so we could trust his judgement. Before we took off that night, he also inspected our 'chutes to check their reliability and to make sure they had been correctly packed. We were all wearing low-level, square 'chutes — GQ360s to be accurate — a square parachute with 360sq ft of material. These 'chutes had to support the weight of a full-grown, 6ft-tall man weighing around 180lb and a further 120lb of equipment. The great asset about the low-level 'chutes is their high manoeuvrability. One of the reasons for the secret night trials that weekend was to test new RIBs in windy conditions, and the wind that evening had been gusting at around 28 knots, when no peace-time jump is permitted at higher than 15 knots! We hoped the 'met' boys were accurate with their forecast.

We were briefed by the scientists at around eight o'clock that evening and told there would be eight practice jumps, so that all the scientists on board would be able to evaluate the problems and test the new equipment under different conditions.

'Because of the fact that these jumps must be made over water,' explained the chief scientist, 'you will all have to wear wet-suits ...'

There was a quiet chorus of complaint, and

the scientist looked up.

'Pardon?' he said.

'Well, Sir,' said one of the SBS crew, 'it is very hot tonight and in those wet-suits we will be sweltering.'

Someone else piped up, 'You must be taking the piss, gentlemen; it will be hell in those suits in this weather.'

But we were joking. We knew we would have to wear the wet-suits but we would have preferred to jump that night in trunks. We knew the water was warm and we would have enjoyed a pleasant swim. It wasn't to be. Despite our jocular mood this was, of course, a serious, scientific exercise. We were, in fact, dressed in black wet-suits, black diving hoods and black jungle boots, with black fins attached to the shins. But we were carrying no weapons, which was a relief. Two camera crews would be working alongside us that night, one crew on the C130 with night-vision cameras and another crew in a Chipmunk flying alongside, making sure all the angles were covered so the scientists could judge how well the experiment had gone.

The take-off from Boscombe Down and the flight was uneventful and we were all in position to jump in plenty of time. Visibility was excellent but the pilot reported that the wind speed had increased once more and was once again gusting in excess of 30 knots. He believed there was a real possibility of the wind speed increasing, if anything. We thought that meant the jump would be postponed, we would return to Boscombe Down and start the experiment again the next day. But the decision was taken by God knows whom to carry on that night and take the risk.

The RIB was deployed successfully out of the rear of the Hercules and we heard the whoosh of wind as the RIB sped out of the back of the plane in seconds. As directed, we all followed in quick succession. We knew the wind would make the jump from 1,500ft very tricky but we had jumped in worse conditions. SBS parachutists were renowned for jumping in the most difficult, some would say almost impossible, weather conditions. I was second to last of the ten Marines to jump and everything went fine. I checked my canopy after the mandatory three-second count and the 'chute opened perfectly. I looked all round me, making sure I was not about to collide with anyone else, and then I checked the target RIB which seemed to be some distance away. I had enough time to take in the wonderful view with the almost full moon overhead making the night sky bright and stunning.

Then I looked down and realised that the wind was blowing me off course and, at this rate of knots, I was pretty certain that I hadn't a cat in hell's chance of landing in the water. What worried me was how far inland the wind would take me. I hoped that I would be able to manoeuvre the 'chute to land on the beach but I wasn't sure I would be able to do so. Beyond the beach I had no idea what to expect, but I suspected there would be unwelcome houses which would be no joke. No parachutist wants to end up slamming into the side of a building at a rate of knots.

I could see the RIB had landed in the water, but instead of being three miles from the shore it had actually ended up only about 50ft from the beach. I could see the others all heading for the beach and beyond, and it seemed that no one would actually make it into the water but would all end up somewhere on dry land. Desperately, I tried to adjust my 'chute to ensure I would drop in the water, but the gusts of wind were far too strong. I saw one jumper, whom I presumed to be John, disappearing from view and judged he must have landed about a mile inland. There was nothing left to do now but trust in luck and hope for the best. I was lucky. I managed to land in the grounds of the hotel quite safely, but my 'chute did become entangled in some of the hotel's garden furniture.

When I had gathered in my canopy I looked around at the reception. A hundred or more people, all dressed in their wedding gear, were gazing at us from the safety of the marquee wondering what on earth was going on. Some thought it was all part of a stunt, a wild kind of surprise for the bride and groom. Others were somewhat taken aback at seeing ten men dressed in black, and looking distinctly menacing, invading their wedding reception from the sky. Hearing the screaming and the commotion, those people who had been staying and drinking in the hotel came running out to see what was happening.

Then the jokes began. 'Where's the Milk Tray?' was the favourite because everyone had seen the advertisement on television.

Others asked, somewhat brusquely, 'What the hell's going on? What are you lot playing at? Who the hell are you?'

Hurriedly, the five of us who had landed around the marquee started to apologise and explain, but we were missing five of our team. We had little time for niceties because we were worried about our mates. Of course, no one present had the vaguest idea who or what we were or what we were doing in the middle of their wedding party. But we needed to find our mates and quickly, fearful one or more may have been seriously injured and might need urgent hospital treatment.

'Have you seen any more dressed like us?' we asked, and people began looking around and asking each other the same question.

We quickly gathered that some people had seen others sailing over the hotel roof and disappearing. We knew there was a main road by the hotel and, beyond that, some thick woodland. We just hoped there weren't any overhead power cables.

I ran to a cottage in the grounds, pushed open the door and asked a couple if they had seen a parachutist descending nearby. Somewhat taken aback, the man replied, 'What are you doing in our cottage dressed like that? Get out before I call the police.'

Of course I apologised and told him there had been a terrible mistake; that a group of Royal Marines had been blown off course and had landed near his cottage. But he still didn't look very pleased when I made my apologies and left.

As I ran back towards the marquee to see if any of the others had been found, a girl came up to me. 'Wouldn't you like a drink before you go off again? I'm sure your friend will be fine.'

I'm afraid I wasn't very polite.

'Shit, no,' I replied. 'I'm sorry, but one of my mates may have been badly injured. When I've found the others I'd love a drink. Get some beers lined up for us, OK?'

'Right,' she said, 'but don't be long.'

Fifteen minutes later, eight of us were sitting down together in the marquee while an ambulance had taken the two injured Marines to hospital. The landlord came out and brought us pints of beer and told us it was all on the house. The girls began plying us with champagne and the music re-started. Before we could say 'no' we were all quite pissed, and reflecting on what had obviously gone completely wrong.

The police arrived and we explained the situation, and the SBS HQ at Poole was informed that eight of their men dressed in wet-suits were at the hotel in Swanage, while two others had been taken to hospital, suffering superficial injuries. Headquarters said they would immediately send vehicles to pick us up.

As soon as our officers arrived, the police were asked to collect all the cameras and take out the film so that no record could be kept of the drop that had turned into a disaster. Some of the guests weren't too happy handing over their films, as most of the frames had been taken earlier photographing the bride and groom. They were given no option. Before our officers arrived on the scene, however, we had gathered loads of telephone numbers and we told the girls that we would soon be holding a party at our HQ to which all would be invited. A week later, we held a barbecue and invited along seven of the girls. They seemed to have a great evening and so did at least two of our mates, who got lucky with two girls who spent the night in camp.

At the inquest that followed, the trials team began by blaming us for the disaster, describing us as 'crap parachutists' to which we took great exception. After an investigation, however, it was discovered that we had been given the order to go, some 22 seconds too soon with a wind speed of around thirty knots. As a result, it would have been physically impossible to land in the water and, thankfully, we were all exonerated, though the scientists didn't seem too happy. In fact, the reason we landed in the hotel was because we were thrown out 22 seconds too early.

There were other such scrapes and incidents which, at the time, appeared serious, but looking back on them some time later made us realise how funny they were.

In February 1992, we were on a tour of duty at Warren Point in Northern Ireland, patrolling Carlingford Lough below the Mourne Mountains. One of our duties was to keep a watch on the ferries arriving and leaving Warren Point, stopping and searching them for any IRA personnel or arms and ammunition. A team of Marines men would man an RIB and follow the ferries as they left port. Our RIBs were powered by two engines. Then we would order the ferry to stop and board the ships using Jacob's ladders. We would always carry arms and be ready for anyone who tried to stop us searching the ship. We usually took a Springer spaniel 'sniffer' dog with us, too, and he would be pulled on board in a harness.

Generally, we would be dressed in black dry-suits with black woolly hats. We would carry 9mm Browning pistols, MP5s and sometimes H & K 53s with .556 calibre bullets. Once on board, the dog handler would go about his work while we searched the vehicles and all the cabins. By the time we had completed the search, the ferry would be somewhere near the end of the lough. If all was well, we would then disembark back on to the RIB and head for home, a Royal Navy minesweeper where we lived throughout our tour of duty. Sometimes, particularly in winter, the seas would become too rough to disembark on to our RIB and we would have to leap into the icy water, around 40ft below the deck. On those occasions one or two of us would hit the water really hard, knocking the wind out of ourselves. One Marine had to be hospitalised after such a leap, suffering from internal bleeding.

When we weren't patrolling the lough, we would go out on patrols, searching the coastline looking for IRA ammunition and weapons dumps. Sometimes we would team up with SAS troops in the area and undertake deep penetration exercises, where we might lie low undercover for days at a time, keeping watch on suspects.

At around ten-thirty one morning we received a 'May Day' distress signal to go to a Turkish ship that was in Carlingford Lough. A man had been found on board in a serious condition and needed urgent hospital treatment to have any chance of surviving. The weather was atrocious, making a helicopter evacuation from the ship impossible. So eight of us were despatched in an RIB with orders to board the vessel, check out the man and, if necessary, escort him back to shore where an ambulance would be waiting.

When we finally boarded and secured the ship, which was carrying about 400 head of cattle, we discovered that the man, the ship's radio operator, had died. Apparently, four hours earlier, the man, who was in his forties, had suffered a severe heart-attack. He had never recovered consciousness. But getting him off the ship proved difficult because no chopper could make the trip in such rough weather. In the end, six of us had to put the man, who weighed over 16 stone, in a body bag and lower him on to the RIB that was riding the waves below. Then we headed back to port and found the Coroner who was waiting for us.

When we had finally hauled the body on to the

dockside, we met the Coroner.

'Where's your van?' we asked. 'We'll carry him over for you.'

'I have a problem there,' said the Coroner in a broad Irish accent.

'What's that?' we asked.

'I've no Coroner's van,' he explained. 'It's broken down.'

'What are we going to do then?' someone asked.

'I've brought my wife's car,' he said, 'we'll have to put him in that.'

'But he's too big to go in the boot,' we argued.

'Don't worry about that,' he replied, 'We'll just put him in the front seat and prop him up as though he's going for a nice ride. Anyone who sees him will just think he's a passenger having a sleep.'

We hauled the body over to the car and with great difficulty managed to squeeze the man into the front seat.

'You can't leave him like that,' said the Coroner. 'Take him out of the body bag and I'll put a hat on his head. It'll look more natural.'

And we did just that. Five minutes later, the Coroner was driving through town on his way to the mortuary with a dead stranger sitting next to him, sitting upright with a hat on his head and his seat-belt securely holding him in place.

In March 1993, we were on patrol in Kilkeel, Northern Ireland, detailed to carry out two weeks' patrolling on the streets of Belfast and then two weeks' patrolling Carlingford Lough. It was some time shortly after five o'clock in the afternoon and we were all dying for a cup of tea. We tied up the Rigid Raider and decided to stretch our legs after a nine-hour stint of duty in the boat. We were suffering from cramp and muscle stiffness. We were dressed in army fatigues and carrying our British Army-issue SA80 weapons. We were also wearing our famous black woolly hats.

Unknown to us, we had, in fact, just been sighted by a British Army patrol who believed we were an IRA active service unit on patrol. They reached this conclusion primarily because we were wearing our black woolly hats and old army fatigues which many IRA active service units also wore. The British patrol were about to open fire on us and had, in fact, cocked their GP machine-gun ready to take us out when there was an almighty crash near their position.

They realised that they themselves had come under attack from a totally different direction with mortar bombs raining down on them as they had taken up their positions preparing to target us. The IRA was firing the mortar bombs at a Royal Irish Regiment of about 60 men who were camped on a football pitch next to the local school where a detachment of Marines were stationed.

Within a matter of minutes, the extraordinary situation had been analysed and some 24 Marines and Irish Rangers had been ordered to burst out of the camp and make for the spot where the mortars were being fired. They burst out, spreading into a 'star' formation as soon as they were out of the school gates. Armed only with SA80s and MP5s, the men raced towards the spot and found the base plate of a mortar gun inside a Ford Sierra car with the roof neatly cut out. The intention was to track down and capture the IRA unit and, if they didn't surrender, take them out.

Other Royal Irish Rangers were ordered to throw a cordon around the school and secure the area. The bomb squad were called in because it was feared that some of the mortars had landed inside the school but had not exploded. Many such IRA mortar bombs were extremely dangerous because they were usually home-made and therefore very insecure, liable to explode at any moment. Understandably, British bomb-disposal squads treated such bombs with great caution.

During the casualty assessment which followed, we suddenly realised that one of the lads was missing and no one had any idea where the hell he could have been. It was established that he had not left the camp and we feared that he may have been hit by one of the mortars that hadn't exploded on impact. Thirty minutes later, the bomb squad moved through the school, gingerly examining and clearing each room, taking no chances. We had not been permitted to enter the building for fear of accidentally setting off one of the unexploded bombs.

One mortar bomb had, in fact, gone through the gymnasium roof, but no one had recalled it exploding. Gingerly, the bomb squad moved in and they could see the unexploded bomb quite clearly lying on the floor. Only six feet away from the bomb was our missing man, lying naked under a sunbed with his Walkman clamped to his ears, utterly oblivious to the events of the last hour. Even now, as he lay there, soaking up the rays and sound asleep, he was unaware that an unexploded bomb was only a few feet away. If the bomb had exploded, he would have been killed.

Gingerly, the bomb squad moved in behind a protective, reinforced blast blanket, inching their way towards the sleeping Marine. Then, without ceremony, they grabbed the Marine, threw the blanket over him and dragged him forcibly out of the room while he screamed and yelled.

'What the fuck are you doing?' he was yelling over and over again. 'What the fuck do you think you are playing at?'

'Shut up, keep quiet,' the bomb squad yelled at him.

But he was wild, fighting and kicking at the men trying to save his life. Eventually, they succeeded in dragging him out of the room to safety and explained to him precisely what had happened. At first, he refused to believe their explanation, thinking they were simply having a joke at his expense. After all, he had heard nothing. Then they let him see the mortar bomb lying a few feet from the sunbed and he turned white. He never forgot that incident and neither did we. But he took it all in good heart and later bought the bomb squad lads a few pints of beer.

There were other, more dangerous events which, after the trauma and emotional shock had passed, we would end up having a damn good belly laugh about. One such incident occurred in Northern Ireland during the height of the Troubles when we were on our two-weekly tour of duty patrolling West Belfast.

It was some time in December 1992, and we were tasked to re-supply and re-distribute arms, ammunition and equipment around the Province. After a hard night's drinking, consuming large quantities of dry cider in a NAAFI just outside Belfast, the five Royal Marines and four SAS men detailed to move the equipment clambered bleary-eyed into a Ford Transit van for the drive from Belfast to Warren Point. On board were 2,000 rounds of ammunition and communications equipment, as well as the nine of us who were all armed with MP5s and Heckler & Koch 53s. Behind us was an armed escort, four-wheel-drive Daihatsu, carrying a few men, each armed with a 9mm Browning, one MP5 and an SA80 rifle. They also carried some smoke grenades, flares and a full medical kit. This re-supply trip was always considered a dangerous run because we had to pass through the bandit country of South Armagh over which the IRA had virtual control. Indeed, for the most part, this area of Northern Ireland was out of bounds to all British servicemen unless undertaking special missions, which had to be approved at the highest British Army authority in the Province.

We were gently moving through Belfast's rush-hour traffic a little after eight-thirty in the morning, driving through the city centre and out towards the M1. We had passed the cemetery and were slowly approaching the infamous Divis block of flats, which meant we had to change channels on our secure radio which was concealed under the dashboard. I had just bent down to alter the radio channel to the new frequency when there was an almighty crash and I was thrown forward, my nose smashing into the dashboard, which sent a wave of pain searing through my head. The blood spurted from my nose, covering the floor, but in that instant I was more concerned about what had happened to the vehicle. I was worried. Had we been hit accidentally or had we been deliberately rammed by another vehicle? As I looked up, I realised that we had driven into the back of a huge articulated truck.

'What the fuck's happened?' I asked the driver, because when we hit the truck my head was below the dashboard at the time.

'I've just crashed the van,' said the driver, 'went straight into the back of it.'

The truck driver stopped his vehicle and walked to the back to check the damage we had caused. Our driver got down from the Transit and went to inspect the front of the vehicle. Fortunately, there was no damage to the truck, but the radiator of our Transit had been punctured and the water and anti-freeze was all over the road. We obviously needed to get our van off the road to ease the traffic flow, so we moved the van on to the grass verge.

We immediately called up our HQ to report the accident, telling him we had skidded on some diesel which had spilt on to the road. We needed a recovery vehicle as soon as possible because we were sitting ducks. We had broken down in West Belfast, where we knew every other male over the age of 16 was either a member of the IRA, an IRA sympathiser or a staunch Republican. We would have made an easy target for anyone who decided that this was a heaven-sent opportunity to cause trouble, if not take out a few British Army personnel. We felt totally exposed because we thought it was obvious we were British Army, despite being dressed in jeans, T-shirts and trainers. And the fact that a back-up vehicle was immediately behind us also gave the game away to any half-bright IRA member.

Inside the Transit, we held a quick council of war and made a plan of action which we would put into effect in case we had been compromised, and one or two local lads tried to take us out. We all cocked our personal weapons and checked the magazines, as well as the spares we all carried. If attacked, we planned to use the vehicle as a defence and try to frighten off the gunmen, but we knew we would have to be careful because there were a great number of civilians and innocent people about, as well as a stream of traffic passing by. We also had 2,000 rounds in the van, which we had no intention of letting the IRA get their hands on. If the situation became desperate and we found ourselves under attack from various quarters, then we decided we would have to make a fighting withdrawal. We had practised such withdrawals a hundred times and knew precisely what to do. But that action would only be taken as a last resort. We believed with the weapons and ammunition at our disposal, we would be able to hold our own against quite a force.

We decided to split our meagre manpower. Three of us decided to make our breakdown look as ordinary and normal as possible, so we got out of the vehicle, lifted the bonnet and then lay around on the grass, trying to look as nonchalant as possible and, at the same time, keeping our eyes peeled for any suspicious characters. Before getting out of the van, I stuffed my hip pistol in my jeans and, thankfully, my T-shirt covered the bulge on my hip. I also took my duffle bag and put an SA80 rifle inside and three smoke grenades. I wrapped my loaded MP5 in a jacket and laid that on the ground beside me. The others stayed in the vehicle with their weapons and the ammunition. Although we maintained radio silence, it was kept open for any messages. Then we all settled down to wait.

Two hours passed and there was no sign of any recovery vehicle. We decided we should call the RUC and tell them what had happened, giving details of our position. It was decided they would put out a few patrols in and around the immediate area in the hope of frightening away any IRA personnel who might have decided to take action against us. They believed that if they were seen patrolling the area, any IRA plan of attack might be averted.

Four hours later, a civilian recovery vehicle, manned by REME engineers arrived, hitched up the Transit and drove us back to the barracks we had left hours earlier. But our driver had to pay the penalty for putting us in such a risky situation. We decided he had to buy four rounds of cider, one round for every hour we had been forced to wait on tenterhooks for the IRA to launch an attack against us. He had confessed to us during that time that, in fact, there had been no accident; he had fallen asleep at the wheel of the Transit after drinking eight pints of cider and then spending the rest of the night shagging his girlfriend. He also had to pay a £30 fine to the Army for driving carelessly, but we never told the authorities the real reason we had crashed.

Such camaraderie was everyday practice in the Special Boat Service. None of us would ever let down a mate in trouble and each and every one of us would support any SBS soldier on any occasion, whether it was a fist-fight in a bar or a life-and-death military action against an armed enemy.

But there were exceptions.

And those exceptions, which have never before been revealed, took place in a small, single-storey, flat-roofed, windowless brick building next to a store room at the Royal Marine headquarters in Poole Harbour. The single room measured approximately 25ft by 15ft and along one side was a makeshift bar. The floor was bare and wooden, and it was furnished with a couple of tables and some wooden chairs. The place was known affectionately as the Frog Inn, so named because of the 'Frog' symbol which adorns the SBS insignia. It also contains many of the souvenirs and memorabilia of the SBS going back to World War II. And the only people permitted entry into the Frog were members of the Special Boat Service, both officers, NCOs and men. No women were permitted.

It was inside the Frog Inn that officers, NCOs and soldiers of the Special Boat Service let down their hair and on many occasions became wonderfully, hopelessly, paralytically drunk. On those occasions there were no ranks, no authority and no seniority. Everyone was equal and people took the piss out of each other as much as they liked without fear or favour. To some extent, the atmosphere of the Frog Inn helped to mould together every member of the SBS as a cohesive, single-minded fighting force, instilling extraordinary comradeship and trust in each other. We all realised that what went on inside the Frog Inn could never be accepted outside, where the Unit was a tough, highly disciplined organisation demanding the highest standards. When we walked out of the Frog Inn, no matter how drunk and incapable we had become, the atmosphere changed and we all returned to the accepted disciplines that have to exist between officers, NCOs and men. But inside that ordinary brick building, there were no holds barred.

The Frog Inn is the place where the SBS meet to celebrate and commemorate. When a task has been successfully carried out, the SBS gather there to unwind, which usually entails getting blind drunk. But it is also the place where everyone gathers if an SBS man is killed in action or in training, where we can get together to discuss what happened and, if necessary, vent our rage or our sadness over the death of one of us. We liked to get away, to be together on such occasions, away from the families and the formalities, so that we could grieve in our own way.

Besides those special and sad occasions, it was normal practice to spend at least one afternoon or evening at the Frog Inn when we were in camp at Poole. We all worked and trained damned hard and we looked forward to the escape the Frog Inn permitted where barrels of our favourite drink — Guinness — would be downed in a good session by perhaps 20 or 30 men hell-bent on getting pissed. To make matters worse, someone might also produce a few bottles of Bacardi or Scotch to give the Guinness more oomph. And during most sessions, the 'yard' glass would be produced from behind the bar and a number of Marines would have to undergo the test to see if they were capable of drinking the yard without once removing the glass from the lips. Of course, most of us ended up pouring the last pint or so down our chests, but the men who could simply open their gullets and pour the liquid down were always the winners, downing it all faster than mere mortals. Sometimes I wondered how our heads managed to cope with the extraordinary intake of alcohol. And yet, the next morning we would all be on parade or taking part in training exercises that would test the toughest, most athletic men. And there was no shirking.

But the best kept secret of the Frog Inn — known only to SBS personnel — were the totally unofficial Kangaroo Courts which were held there from time to time. These were great fun for everyone taking part except for the poor, unfortunate victim — the prisoner at the bar. For him the outcome was nearly always extremely painful.

After perhaps two or three hours of heavy drinking, someone would have the bright idea of criticising a colleague for no apparent reason. The criticism could be as trivial as someone snoring too much while asleep, being too argumentative with his mates or, most importantly, missing a piss-up. But no matter how trivial the charge, if the mood in the room that day was for a trial to be held, then the poor bastard didn't stand a chance. No one ever had to answer to a serious charge of making a mistake in training or on exercise — on the contrary, it was always good, clean, fun, with the prisoner having to answer flippant charges.

The court would be arranged and a table put in front of the judge's chair. Anyone could be appointed judge, no matter what his rank. Prosecution and defence counsel would be selected, over which the accused man had no control. Both sides would bring forward witnesses and the rest of those present in the bar would act as the jury. The prisoner would sit in the middle of the room facing the judge.

Most of the trials would last around 15 minutes, which was mainly spent with the prosecution and defence making jokes — frequently very crude and rude — about the accused. The rest of the lads would cheer and shout encouragement whenever a good, convincing piece of evidence was made against the poor prisoner in the dock.

One Royal Marine named Stan had a reputation for being a 'tight-wad' — very careful with his money. It was decided he should stand trial, accused of being a 'stingy, tight-fisted bastard'. The court was set up and the judge called Stan to sit in the dock.

'Are you guilty or not guilty of the charge of stinginess made against you?' asked the judge.

'Not guilty,' replied Stan.

The first witness called to give evidence was asked why he thought that Stan was a stingy bastard.

'Well, Your Honour,' he began, 'on the afternoon in question we had just finished work and were pretty knackered so me and another Marine named Tim asked Stan to give us a lift home in his car. Stan agreed so we left camp in his car. I happen to live a couple of miles further away from camp than Stan and Tim and when they dropped me Stan asked for £1 to pay for the extra petrol he had to use driving me an extra two miles. I began to laugh, Your Honour, but threw Stan a £1 coin before going into my house for tea. But that proves he is a tight-fisted bastard.'

The room erupted into laughter and cheers and Stan seemed annoyed that the court case appeared to be going against him.

Another witness told how he had volunteered to go to the fish and chip shop and when he returned, Stan asked for the six pence change that was due to him.

Then Stan called for defence witnesses. One mate recalled how Stan had once lent him £8.50 to go shopping. There were boos around the bar and it seemed that Stan was going to be found not guilty.

Then the witness held up his hand and the judge asked him to continue. He said, 'A few days later, Stan asked me for a £10 note in payment for the loan of £8.50. When I reminded him he had only lent me £8.50, he said that didn't matter, demanding the £10 which he claimed included the interest owed on the loan.' There was a roar of approval from all the lads and shouts of 'guilty, guilty'. That piece of evidence was sufficient to prove Stan's guilt and he was sentenced to a paddling.

Stan was grabbed from behind and frog-marched to the table. He was forcibly bent over the table and someone took down his trousers and pants and lifted his shirt so that his arse was totally bare. Then the 'Lord High Executioner' was called forward and he arrived with a black balaclava over his head and wielding a large, 4ft-long wooden Gemini boat paddle that was always used to punish anyone found guilty in the Frog Kangaroo Court.

'Thwack.' The dark green paddle was brought down with brute force striking Stan across his bare backside with real ferocity. Five times the paddle was brought down with the same ferocity and Stan looked as though he was about to pass out. Tears came into his eyes every time the paddle 'thwacked' him and he was moaning with the pain that must have been truly horrendous. Those Gemini paddles are large and robust and the Executioner was a strong man who put everything into handing out the punishment. Stan

279 / NOT BY STRENGTH BY GUILE

279 / *NOT BY STRENGTH BY GUILE*

straightened up after the fifth hit and everyone cheered. His backside was red raw from the pounding. He was handed a pint of Guinness but he didn't want to sit down again that afternoon. Stan later confirmed that his backside had been painful for four days and the bruising didn't disappear for nearly two weeks!

Such Kangaroo Courts were held once every couple of weeks and on nearly every occasion the poor prisoner would be sentenced to a paddling. One poor guy looked like he was going to faint from a paddling, but he quickly revived after having a few pints of beer thrown over him. But, though the tanning was always rigourous and hurt like hell, there was no one who ever bottled out of facing up to it.

Not everyone, however, was sentenced to a paddling.

On one occasion, a Royal Marines Captain was ordered to stand trial in the Frog Inn, having been accused of being 'too smooth, of being too well dressed when off duty, of having too nice a car, of having a too good-looking, long-legged, blonde girlfriend and of allegedly using a sun bed'. He refused to have a defence counsel, preferring to defend himself. The prosecution witnesses all gave evidence against the smooth officer, but as no one agreed to appear as a defence witness, he was found guilty as charged. He was sentenced to walk through the camp with a bra on his head and report to the guard room Sergeant, as well as order four pints of the best port from the Officers' Mess and put them on his Mess bill. But he had escaped a paddling.

Some hilarious parties took place in the Frog Inn, which usually ended in a number of Marines becoming really drunk and, occasionally, sick, and they sometimes ended in wild escapades which we would never have dreamed of carrying out when sober.

One day in November 1995, we had carried out a successful job involving three RIBs in the English Channel in the most appalling weather conditions, involving heavy seas and driving rain. Back at base, the Officer Commanding ordered a barrel of Guinness to be delivered to the Frog Inn for a job well done. Within a couple of hours, we were all wrecked and looking for fun.

Someone suggested a naked 'twos-up' bicycle race on mountain bikes from the top camp to the bottom camp, a distance of one-and-a-half miles. One rode the bike while the other stood behind the rider. Everyone was naked. There were nine bikes with 18 naked Marines taking part. When we'd finished the race, we all jumped into the freezing sea and swam around before running back to the Frog to collect our clothes. But locals who were overlooking the road had seen our nude bike race, phoned the barracks guard room and complained about the nakedness and our behaviour.

The Guard Commander, sober and sensible, came down and read the riot act, telling us, 'All of you get dressed otherwise you will all be in the shit. Understand?'

We argued the toss with him and took the piss out of him, but we were sobering up fast and realised we had over-stepped the mark. 'Come on, lads, for fuck's sake,' he said, almost pleading with us, and we went along with that. But it was not the end of the matter. Someone complained of feeling sick and one of his mates grabbed the foam fire-extinguisher and set it off, covering everyone in powder. We looked like naked ghosts.

Then the SBS Captain walked in and looked at us, shaking his head. 'What the hell have you lot been up to?' he exclaimed. 'Now listen to me. I'll go away and pretend I've seen nothing, but if this lot isn't cleaned up by the time I return, the whole lot of you will be for the high jump. Get it?'

We knew he meant it; we also knew that he had given us a chance and we weren't about to fuck it up. Somehow we sobered up enough to clean up the mess, and then made our way unsteadily to bed.

On another occasion during a barbecue outside the Frog, one lad passed out from excess of alcohol. Someone had the bright idea of dismantling his bike and stuffing the seat stem full of sausages and putting the seat back again. We said not a word to the poor bastard but he noticed that the neighbourhood dogs began sniffing around his bike and wouldn't leave it alone. He couldn't understand their interest. A week or so later he, too, could smell the stench, but he had no idea what we had done. Finally, we told him, and he tried to get rid of the rancid sausage meat by using a wire clothes hanger, but the stench never left the bike and the dogs continued sniffing around. Finally, he had no alternative but to sell the bike because he found it impossible to get rid of the smell.

Sometimes, SBS mates took too much of a liberty when pissed out of their minds. At

Christmas 1995, one tall, well-built, good-looking Royal Marine in his mid-twenties went too far. Along with many other Marines, he was attending a bow-tie Christmas dinner dance in a hotel near Bournemouth which was attended by top-brass senior officers, not only from the Royal Marines but also from other regiments. The Royal Marine decided to show off his dancing prowess. He had always fancied himself as a highly successful flirt and as he danced in his drunken state, he began slowly to strip off. People began clapping and encouraging him, including the women present, and the Marine stripped to his underclothes showing off his suntan and strong, athletic physique. The younger women were cheering him on, giggling and shouting 'get them off'. To everyone's surprise, he did just that. He took off his boxers and threw them in the air, before posing totally naked in the middle of the floor, dancing like a gorilla with his arms flapping everywhere.

'Get him out of here,' one of the bosses said to some of us.

The officers present were embarrassed for some of the older women present, and they had no wish to see a drunken, naked Marine showing off in this way, bringing the regiment into disrepute, though they realised it was all in good fun. But he had gone too far. We ran on to the dance floor, grabbed hold of him and his clothes, dragged him out of the ballroom and poured him into a taxi, throwing his clothes after him. Totally embarrassed, his wife refused to go with him, preferring to stay behind and apologise to everyone for her husband's outrageous behaviour. The following day he was fined £150 for bringing the SBS into disrepute. The money went into Troop funds.

But the matter didn't end there. During the next rave-up at the Frog, the Marine was ordered to attend the Kangaroo Court and charged with having too small a cock, showing off in public and making the CO's wife jealous. The prosecution witnesses gave graphic details of the night's events and the Marine was ordered to be given a harsh paddling by the hooded Executioner. As a result, he suffered a painful beating and a sore, severely bruised arse which hurt for ten days.

I had a reputation in the SBS for getting into scrapes but managing to escape real trouble, though I was fined on a number of occasions for 'outrageous behaviour'. On one occasion I was fined £200 — the money going to Troop funds —

for what the Commanding Officer described graphically as 'urban surfing'.

A few of us had been out for a night's drinking in Scotland and were returning to barracks in a 4-ton truck. Two of us decided to play silly buggers, so we climbed on to the canvas roof of the army truck as it thundered through the night back to camp. It was, of course, a stupid and dangerous escapade, but we didn't think of that at the time. We held on for our very lives as the truck hurtled round bends, though the driver had no idea we were on top of the vehicle and hanging on for grim death.

As we approached the guard room, one Marine noticed the feet of my mate hanging over the back of the roof, shouted to the driver to halt and pulled my mate down, marching him off to the guard room. I thought I had escaped, but as the truck moved away and drove up the hill, the Duty Guard Officer saw me lying flat on the top of the vehicle and phoned our Duty Officer. When we had all disembarked, we were ordered to fall in while the officer told us that if the person seen on top of the truck didn't own up, then the entire troop would have to stand out in the freezing cold throughout the night.

'Whoever was on top of that vehicle should own up,' said the Duty Officer. 'He won't get into trouble, but will only receive a telling-off for being such a stupid prat.'

I owned up immediately.

Minutes later I found myself facing a disciplinary hearing for taking part in a dangerous prank.

'But you said that whoever owned up would only get a telling-off,' I said to the officer.

'Well I was fucking lying,' he replied straight-faced.

'But I did nothing wrong,' I protested. 'There's nothing in military law against what I did.'

'Let me see,' he said, and proceeded to pick up the Army Manual and read through it.

'Yes there is,' he said. 'Urban surfing. You're guilty of urban surfing.'

'Urban surfing?' I protested again. 'What's that?'

'What you did,' he replied smiling. 'I've just made it up. Good, isn't it?'

I had no reply. I found it difficult not to burst out laughing because I thought it was a very apt description. But I didn't laugh when he fined me £200. However, I knew he was right to fine me, to stop others who from repeating what was really a stupid and dangerous stunt.

I don't know whether it was the fact I was constantly on stand-by, or that I could never plan a holiday properly, or that I was always at the beck and call of the SBS. But I found myself becoming jealous of other people's lives, of their freedom to make their own decisions, or go wherever they wanted without telling anyone, without getting permission. Ever since that wonderful day when I had joined M Squadron and become part of the SBS, I had been on a three-hour stand-by. I found myself becoming anxious that I had no freedom, no time that I could ever call my own, and the more I thought about it, the more I wanted some space to do what I pleased when I wanted.

I was 26 years old and every decision had been taken for me ever since I had joined the Royal Marines. I had enjoyed virtually every minute of it, even the tough times and the rough, hard, relentless physical endurance tests, which I believed had made me a man. I wasn't in any way disillusioned with the Royal Marines. To me, it had always been a privilege to be a member of probably the greatest Special Forces unit in the world. Now I needed to test myself in the world outside the Royal Marines.

And I had been unable to forget my two mates who had died while serving with me. They hadn't died in battle or fighting a war, but in training exercises. These exercises were meant to test us, to train us, not to kill us. I knew that both men had died in accidents — freak accidents — which should never have occurred. But they had happened; my mates had died and for what? I found those thoughts difficult to reconcile, because I knew those exercises were essential.

And my mates would roar with laughter when I told them that the two things I didn't enjoy about the SBS were two of the most vital disciplines — parachuting and diving. I don't know why I had been scared of parachuting, but there was something that made me virtually shit myself every time I had to make a jump. However, I had more or less overcome that fear the more experience I gained. And by the time I came to leave the Service, I had started really to enjoy it, especially the square 'chute jumping which was far more controllable and accurate.

Most of the dives I carried out in training were in awful visibility, where I couldn't even see my hand in front of my nose. I simply hated the muck and the dense, cheerless murky surroundings. But I adored diving in beautiful, clear blue waters off Greece and Turkey. I felt I wanted to do more of that instead.

And there were personal reasons. I had broken up with my girlfriend. She had been a lifeline to the world outside the Service of which I knew so little. The fact that we had split made me feel I wanted a good, long-term relationship with someone; that the time had come to settle down and have a family. The deaths of my mates had also made me feel I should be starting a family, rather than risk leaving this world without any little Mercers to carry on my name, my genes, my particular characteristics. Somehow, I wanted to leave something of me behind. Then I would come to my senses and think, 'Poor little bastards, who the fuck would want to be like me?'

I talked it over with my Commanding Officer and told him how I felt and why I felt like I did. And he understood. He knew exactly what was going through my mind and I repected him for that. He didn't try to change my view, to persuade me to stay. I believe he made the right decision. He advised me to take a break, to take time out for up to two years and see if I really could enjoy life in civvy street. But he also made me feel good about the decision I intended to take. He told me that I had been a good Marine, an asset to the Special Boat Service and that because of my first-class service record I could rejoin the Marines without taking the basic training. The only stipulation was that I would have to return to the Service within two years, otherwise I would have to start all over again.

In many ways, I left the SBS with a heavy heart and the worst hangover of my life, but I knew I was taking the right decision, even if I would go crawling back within a few months. When I drove out of the barracks for the last time, I left with great confidence, believing I would have the most fantastic life in the big wide world. But civvy street had some nasty shocks in store for me.

CHAPTER TEN

SOMALIA

The machine-gun opened fire on the front vehicle as we came round the corner at 60mph. I was riding shot-gun in the front passenger seat of the Mercedes and the first rounds took out the windscreen, spraying glass everywhere. Fuck knows where the bullets ended up, but they didn't hit the driver, another ex-Marine called Danny, nor the two European businessmen sitting in the back.

Danny slammed on the brakes and came to a halt by the side of the road as more rounds thudded noisily into the side of the Mercedes.

'Get out, get out,' I screamed at the businessmen as I opened my door and threw myself on to the ground while still holding my AK-47. I ran to the side of the road — away from the car — and began returning fire at the bastards who'd targeted us for God knows what reason.

'Get away from the car,' I yelled at the two businessmen. 'Take cover, but not behind the car.'

I saw that Danny, too, had rolled out of the car, taking his Browning 9mm automatic pistol with him and he ran like hell to the other side of the road before taking cover.

'Lie down, lie down,' I shouted at the two men and stupidly they lay down next to each other, making themselves easy targets for the gunmen.

I fired back at our unknown assailants, hoping to draw their fire, trying to determine how many men were firing at us, trying to pinpoint their positions. It was obvious that they had some sort of automatic and I hoped it was only an AK-47 on automatic rather than a more powerful, more accurate, light machine-gun.

Behind us, the other Mercedes came to a screeching halt about 20 yards away, and the other lads in the front followed the same procedure. Our lads got the two other Europeans out of the vehicle and took them to cover away from the car. I didn't know until later that the second car had also taken some direct hits.

For a few moments, the guns fell silent and I strained to pinpoint where the hell the firing had come from.

'Can you see anything?' I yelled at Danny on the other side of the road.

'Fuck all,' he shouted. 'Any luck your side?'

'Nothing,' I yelled.

Within seconds, however, the firing began again and this time it soon became obvious that we were facing between five and eight men, all firing in our direction. It seemed, thank God, that most of their fire was aimed at the cars. Maybe they hadn't seen us dive out of them and run for cover. I returned fire at one position from which I could see automatic shots and when that fell silent I turned my attention to another site. I reloaded my AK with another magazine and began firing single shots.

Suddenly I heard a burst of automatic fire and realised that this was coming from a new direction, from our left. It was obvious we had to get the hell out of this place as quickly as possible. We had heard of such stories in the weeks we had been in Mogadishu, the Somalian capital, which was in the desperate throes of a civil war being fought out on the streets by what seemed to be a number of rival gangs rather than two rival armies.

We still had no idea who or why anyone was firing at us, but realised that we were up against more than just a couple of guys trying to hijack our vehicles.

I yelled back at Dave who had been driving the second Mercedes. 'Withdraw, withdraw. You take the second vehicle while we return fire.'

'Roger,' shouted Dave.

I yelled to Danny to move first and I started to fire intermittently, giving him the chance to race back ten yards and take up another position behind some cover.

I called to the two Europeans, who were looking petrified lying on the ground as though waiting for bullets to hit them. As soon as Danny had started firing again, I told the two men to run back, separately, going to different sides of the road and then find cover and lie low once again. After they had moved to new positions, I fired a few more rounds and then ran back like hell taking up a position some ten yards behind Danny.

The lads in the other car had returned to their vehicle and made a 'J' turn in the road. The two Europeans in their vehicle had clambered back in, lying on the back seat. We had to hold off the gunmen while making sure our two blokes were safely aboard the rear car before we could think of making good our escape.

I just hoped that those attacking us didn't have the sense to surround us because then we would really have been in the shit. This way, using a fighting withdrawal technique which we had practised time and again during our training in the Marines, we knew there was a better than even chance that we would escape unharmed.

Once more, Danny ran back while I covered him, firing at the invisible men. Some of the time the fire-power they were putting down was quite intense and then it would stop altogether for a minute or so, presumably while they all changed magazines. I yelled at our two Europeans to make a run for it back to the car, telling them to get in and lie low. Then I ran back while Danny took over covering my arse.

We had nearly made it back to the car when six Somalis came out from behind the huts all firing together as they realised we were about to make our getaway. They were dressed in fatigues and wore no helmets or any protective gear. Some even had bandoliers around their chests, looking like Mexican desperadoes. But those guns were real and so were the bullets hitting the ground all around us. I realised that if we didn't get out of this place sharpish, there was a real chance one of their rounds would puncture the fuel tanks and perhaps the tyres as well. But on the plus side, they were firing indiscriminately, hardly bothering to take aim. I wondered at the time whether they were on ganja (the Hindi word for marijuana). If that had been the case, there was every chance we would escape without a scratch.

Finally, there was a lull in the firing and we took that opportunity to run for the car, leaving the other one behind. Danny was already within spitting distance of the car and the two Europeans were safely inside. Danny slammed in another magazine and yelled to me to run for it. He began firing at the advancing gunmen while I raced towards the car. The driver already had the engine revving and the car was moving slowly, weaving from side to side, when I jumped into the back. It was awfully crowded in that car but no one cared a damn as we sped away, accelerating as fast as possible out of trouble. One of the lads looked back to see the gunmen firing jubilantly into the air as they danced around the empty car we had left behind. From their viewpoint, they had achieved a major victory, for there was no chance that we would ever see that Merc again and they would make a tidy profit from selling it on.

Those five minutes were the closest we came to real trouble during the four weeks we were in Mogadishu, employed on a day rate to protect the four European businessmen who were trying to make a million out of the total mess that was Somalia in 1996. As I lay on top of those two guys in the back of the Merc that day, I smiled to myself, wondering how the hell I had managed to get into such a scrape. I was 3,000 miles from home in a lawless African city, where everyone seemed to carry a gun and there was no way of telling who were the good guys and who were the baddies.

I had been at home waiting for the phone to ring, offering me a job on a North Sea oil rig, when an old mate of mine, an ex-Marine named Jonah, asked me whether I fancied earning some really good money working for a British company who wanted to send out a team of former Marines as 'security advisers' to groups of European businessmen working in Somalia.

I had been out of the Marines for a few months and after the thrill and the responsibility of being the coxswain in charge of an RIB, life seemed pretty dull in civvy street. The North Sea job had sounded interesting, but I missed the thrill of action which I had enjoyed so much with the Special Boat Service. To me, that had been the life really worth living. I needed action and loved the feeling of adrenalin pumping through my body, the anticipation of action and excitement.

When Jonah explained the job — and the excellent pay — I was all for the idea. It sounded great. Jonah had been asked to put together a team of 12 including three ex-Paratroopers and three US Special Forces Seals (the US equivalent of the SBS). The pay would be £1,500 a week each in cash for a three-month contract.

As we flew out to Mogadishu on a BA flight, I remember thinking that I would return home three months hence with something like £18,000 in the bank. I had never had that sort of money in my bank account in my life and the thought excited me. I kept dreaming of what I might buy myself; a car, motor-bike or God knows what. It was great to spend the time flying out to Africa wondering how I would spend my anticipated fortune. We landed in Cairo and took a charter flight to Mogadishu. Two Americans had pulled out at the last moment and so we were down to ten men, but that didn't worry us.

On landing, we were driven in taxis to the hotel in Mogadishu and met Dave, a former Para Pathfinder in his mid-thirties, who would be our commanding officer. He was a good guy who understood us all very well. He respected the fact that we were all well-trained special forces soldiers with active service experience. He knew that whatever happened, none of us was likely to panic, no matter how tough the circumstances. We all warmed to him as he seemed to know what was going on and was a born leader.

He had met the four businessmen, three

Brits and a German, and one of them seemed to own the hotel in which we were staying. We were led to believe that the businessmen, who had contacts within the Somali Government, intended to take advantage of the civil war raging in the country, buy up assets cheaply and then sell them off at a good profit some time later. They were prepared to take the risks involved in working in such a dangerous environment, but we soon realised why they needed proper protection. Mogadishu in 1996 was no picnic.

We were given three days to acclimatise to the hot, humid weather. In fact, we spent most of the time getting rat-arsed on the local beer and hanging out in the nightclubs which were really wild. The girls would flock to us in droves and some of the lads went off with them, but I didn't want to know because I had met Clare only a few months before going out to Africa to make my fortune. I didn't want to take any unnecessary risks, despite the fact that some of the girls were absolutely gorgeous and very sexy. Some of the guys thought they were in seventh heaven and couldn't get enough of them.

Apart from the heaving, loud, steaming

nightclubs Mogadishu was a rough, tough African city which seemed to be divided into distinct areas which different war-lords controlled. Most of the young men wandered around carrying AK-47s with a couple of magazines strapped together, but there was no way of telling whether they were government forces or a local militia which owed its allegiance to some renegade war-lord. Fire-fights would break out almost daily at dusk, and we had no intention of getting involved in any such disputes.

And there weren't only gun-fights. The machete still ruled in Somalia and those who roamed the streets wielding that deadly weapon knew exactly how to use them. Hands, arms and legs were chopped off indiscriminately if a band of barbarous, young, machete-wielding thugs came across some hapless individual from a rival splinter group. And over the weeks we stayed in the city, we saw many young people with the most appalling machete wounds over all parts of their bodies. Some seemed to wear such scars with pride. To us, it seemed a sickening business that we wanted nothing to do with. Many of the young soldiers and villains were simply drugged-up teenagers who had been press-ganged as boy soldiers and who had known nothing but war, skirmishes and violence. Their loathing for their enemies was matched only by their hatred of Europeans whom they blamed for all their problems.

Understandably, these armed militias, and even those we thought were government forces, were highly suspicious of the ten Europeans who appeared tough, professional, highly trained mercenaries who walked about carrying 9mm Brownings and AK-47s. But the eyes of those young thugs betrayed their true feelings towards us, a hatred and jealousy that knew no bounds. To many in Mogadishu, we may have looked threatening, but as we only wore jeans and T-shirts it was obvious that we weren't supporting any of the militias which roamed the streets.

From the safety of our hotel, we would hear fire-fights most nights and in the morning when we ventured out we would find the bodies of young men, some in uniforms, others only in jeans and T-shirts, lying in the streets, their bodies ripped open by gunfire. But, of course, there were no weapons around; they had been taken away as booty by whichever faction had carried out the killings. Sometimes we might find 20 or so bodies still lying around after a particularly heavy night of gunfire. The local people would go about their business, shopping in the markets, and take not the slightest notice of the dead bodies which were soon covered by swarms of large, noisy flies. It seemed weird, even surreal. We wondered why no one came to claim the bodies, because they must have been someone's husband, someone's son. But when we returned to the scene later in the day, someone would have taken them away. But each and every time I saw those dead bodies, and realised how cheap life seemed, I was determined to keep my wits about me and not end up like that. I had no wish to end my life on some dirty, dusty, baking street in down-town Mogadishu as breakfast for 1,000 flies.

We met the businessmen — our employers — a couple of days after our arrival. They were typical guys in their forties and fifties who obviously had little or no idea how to handle a gun, let alone protect themselves. None carried a weapon, something we all considered to be a good idea because we feared that if the shit hit the fan, we would probably be more at risk from them than any opposing militia. They provided a Renault Espace, two Mercedes and a Dodge van for our transport, and it was decided that whenever they ventured on to the streets they would have bodyguard protection from us. The vehicles were all in radio contact with our HQ back at the hotel.

We acted like professional bodyguards, checking surroundings for any undesirables before permitting our men to leave the hotel, an office or a factory and get into the vehicle, even though on most occasions the vehicles were parked very close to the exits. We always posted look-outs and made sure that the businessmen were totally protected by us if they ever had to walk any distance in a public place. Most of the time we aimed to keep the businessmen out of sight of the general public. On most days they would only attend one meeting, but that might last for several hours, during which time we wouldn't laze around within spitting distance of the meeting room but would remain alert and watchful for any unwelcome visitors. There were none. It seemed that our very presence frightened off any attempt by a local war-lord against our employers.

Off-duty time was, of course, our own, but most of the time we simply lazed around the hotel. It was a pity there was no swimming pool which would have been great to relax in and keep cool and fit, but no such luck. Instead, we usually stayed in our rooms, watched satellite TV and read the odd book. Food was laid on and there was an efficient room service, but we quickly became bored despite the daily gun battles that would suddenly flare up somewhere around the city and, just as quickly, die down again. We didn't want to know. As the weeks wore on, we became restless and it was sometimes difficult to retain enthusiasm for the job.

Every day, Dave, our friendly CO, would remind us of the pay we were getting for the job we were doing, encouraging us to stay alert, for he could see that our enthusiasm for the job was waning. For the first few weeks after arriving in Somalia, we were woken each night by the sound of gunfire — now I was happily sleeping through all the gun battles, for they had become a boring, nightly occurrence.

Five of us were leisurely strolling back from downing a few beers at the local nightclub, enjoying the beautiful, balmy air and the night sky, when suddenly all hell broke loose. At least four or five people armed with semi-automatics were firing at us from the shadows only 20 yards away.

'Get down,' someone shouted.

'Spread out, spread out,' shouted someone else, as we all hit the ground at once, an instant reaction to the shooting.

I could not see the men firing at us, but I could see the flashes from their guns. I thought they were probably using AK-47s, their favourite weapon. The gunmen seemed to be grouped together behind some cars further down the road, but one was across the street firing at us from a different angle. We were in real shit because we had no weapons with us, nothing at all — not even a commando knife.

I rolled out of the way behind a tree on the pavement, and I could see that my three mates had also hit the ground and taken cover.

'Everyone OK?' shouted Danny and the three of us responded affirmatively. That was the good news. The gunmen had stopped firing but we couldn't see any movement. We had to presume they were changing magazines. But still there was no movement to be seen.

'Anyone see anything?' I yelled and the others replied in the negative.

I decided to draw their fire, to see if the gunmen had decided to walk away after giving us the fright of our lives. I walked out a yard or so from my cover and quickly darted back. Two gunmen fired.

'You OK, Pete?' someone shouted.

'Yes, OK,' I shouted back. 'Just wanted to see if our friends had gone away.'

'Well now you fucking well know,' shouted someone else.

'What's our plan?' someone shouted.

Suddenly I saw one of the gunmen run from his cover to join the man who had been firing at us on his own from the left. He was holding an AK-47. It seemed they were trying to surround us.

'Eleven o'clock,' I shouted, hoping the others would see the gunman and track his movements.

Someone suggested we should plan to make a withdrawal as quickly as possible, but I realised we must have been nearly half-a-mile from the hotel. If these jokers were intent on robbing us — and probably killing us in the process — we had no chance of making the safety of the hotel before being hit.

Suddenly, at least two gunmen opened up on our position and we saw two more gunmen leave the safety of the darkness and run around to the right of us. They, too, were carrying AK-47s.

'Shit,' I thought, 'now we're really in trouble.'

Mick came sprinting over to me and thank God no one opened fire.

'How the fuck are we going to get out of this one?' he said.

'It's no good running, we would never make it,' I said.

'Fuckin' right,' he said.

'What do you think?'

'What about trying to take them?' I asked.

'Do you think we could?' he asked, sounding enthusiastic.

'Don't see why not. They can't be that shit hot.'

As we were trying to decide what the fuck to do, we could see a couple of cars in the distance moving towards our position where we were trapped, and that gave me an idea. But before I could formulate a plan, the cars turned left and disappeared. We were pinned down in a side-road about a quarter-of-a-mile or so from the nightclub, in no-man's-land. There were five or six boarded-up shops to the right and the odd tree on the dusty, well-trodden, sun-baked dirt track that passed for a pavement. The road had been tarred with a strip down the middle for vehicles and the sides of the road had a couple of large flood drains to take away the torrential rains that struck the city for two or three months each year.

I cursed myself that we hadn't taken more notice of our surroundings because we had trodden that route from the hotel to the nightclub on more than a dozen occasions. We hoped our friends were only intending to rob us, but we also knew that every night a dozen or so people, and sometimes a lot more, would end up dead on the streets of the city. Whatever our plan of escape, we had to ensure we did not give these bastards any opportunity to take a pot-shot at us.

What we desperately needed were weapons. Anything would do. Mick went with Jock and while one searched behind the shops for any substantial sticks, or anything at all suitable, the other kept guard in case there were more desperadoes out there looking for trouble. Mick found a strong, 4ft-long piece of wood and he smashed it against a tree to see if it would stand up to serious treatment. It did.

Three of us held a council of war while the other two kept watch. We decided to see if the gunmen were intent on surrounding us. If they still seemed to be trying to do so, we intended to move away a little and then set a trap. All we needed was to grab one of the gunmen and hope he had a few full magazines. Then we would show the fuckers. Danny called out quietly that the men were still moving towards us, obviously intent on surrounding us. We decided to put our plan into operation. Thank God we had all been trained, highly trained, in unarmed combat. When the shit hits the fan, the training takes over. We all knew that if we could get within striking distance of these bastards, they would be dead men.

We moved back and took up our positions watching the right flank, because the two or three men on that side were the ones making their way towards our position. The others began putting down intermittent fire, which made us believe that these gunmen were probably former army servicemen who at least knew something about tactics. That worried me, but we had been used to such strategies in training.

Three of us took cover in darkness behind some sheds ten yards behind the shops. The other two waited behind some vegetation nearby, and Mick, the strongest of us all, held the stick. Every time the gunmen opened fire, we saw movement and realised that only two men were trying to get behind our position. That was good. We watched, holding our breath as they came towards the shops, stopping and crouching down every few yards, waiting for their mates to open up again, giving them an opportunity to get nearer. Nearer and nearer they came. They were both carrying guns, one with an AK-47, the other with a World War II Lee Enfield .303. They were dressed in tattered army fatigues. We couldn't tell how old they were but, by the way they moved, they were probably in their twenties.

When they had nearly drawn level with us, I made a noise like a cat and, instinctively, the two gunmen turned towards me. In that instant,

Mick and Danny leapt from their hideout; Mick smashing one man as hard as he could across the back of the head, knocking him to the ground. But Danny's target turned and was about to open fire when Danny lunged headlong into him, head-butting him in the stomach and knocking the breath out of him. Then Danny hit him, a karate blow to the side of the neck, as he lay on the ground. The man didn't move. We grabbed both their guns, took their magazines, checked to see how many rounds we had and went back to our positions in the darkness. We wanted to determine whether the other gunmen had heard the scuffle, and whether they intended to come searching for their mates.

Shouting began and, of course, no reply was forthcoming. Their two comrades lay still on the path, out cold, if not dead. After a while, the shouting stopped and there was silence. We waited for five minutes and could see no movement, and the firing had stopped completely. We decided to risk it and move out one at a time while others covered us with the rifles. We stealthily moved from one dark spot to another, taking cover wherever possible. We were taking no risks. But it seemed our gun-toting friends had decided not to take any further risks either that night. We never saw or heard anything more. But we were mightily relieved when we finally reached our hotel. We never knew the fate of the two men we had attacked and didn't report the incident to anyone. But it had been a salutary lesson. In future, we took far greater care when venturing out at night, always taking a hotel taxi we knew we could trust.

Shortly after this escapade, the security situation deteriorated rapidly throughout the city. Our employers were becoming more jittery every time we ventured out to a meeting and it seemed it would not be too long before they would call it a day. We had only been in Somalia a little more than a month, but it had become obvious that the entire city could erupt in a major civil war at any time. As a result, we practised our escape plan to the airport if the decision was taken to flee the city. We all knew exactly what we would do and what precautions we would take. Our first priority, of course, was to protect our employers and then ourselves. We knew that we would be quite capable of taking care of them unless we met real military opposition which, from what we had seen, appeared unlikely. If anyone had tried to stop and rob us when making our way to the airport, we believed it would be one or other of the roving bands belonging to some local war-lord and we felt quite confident that we could take that lot out. We were well armed and had plenty of ammunition. If they wanted a fire-fight, they could have one, but we hoped that nothing like that would occur. When bullets fly, accidents can happen. We hoped our return to the airport would be speedy and without incident. But we had to be prepared for any eventuality.

Nevertheless, we still endured some hairy moments.

One day we were driving in our old, white Peugeot 506 along the dirt roads on the outskirts of Mogadishu, when we came round a corner at 60mph. Strung across the road were a line of children and Mick, who was driving, had to take evasive action, otherwise we would have mowed down ten or more kids and God knows how many might have been killed. Mick slammed on the anchors but the car couldn't take the harsh braking and it skidded sideways into a parked car, clipped the front and rolled. We must have rolled and bounced four or five times before coming to rest about 30 yards from the car we hit but, thank God, we had missed all the children. I scrambled out unhurt except for heavy bruising down one side, but the American Marine sitting next to me had smashed his skull into the steel seat-belt attachment and blood was pouring from a gaping wound. He was out cold. The piece of steel had punctured his temple and smashed into his head. I could see part of his brain where the metal had ripped open his skull. The three others in the car were fine, though battered and bruised.

We knew that if we didn't get the Yank to hospital very, very quickly he would be a goner. But we had seen inside one or two Mogadishu hospitals since our arrival and we had no idea if there were any surgeons left in the city who would have been capable of saving his life. Someone had run off to a local doctor, who eventually arrived at the scene to see what he could do. After examining the man, he told us that we had to get him to hospital as soon as possible if there was any chance of saving his life. He volunteered to take him in his car if we would carry him to his house 100 yards away.

We happily did so but the American looked in a very bad way. We collected what money we had between us, about £200, and gave it to the doctor asking him to take care of our colleague. We took the doctor's name and phone number and then made our way back to the hotel. We heard later that the American had never regained consciousness.

The death of the American seemed like an omen, a warning to get the hell out of Somalia while we could. We listened to the BBC World Service every day and the reports indicated that all-out civil war appeared imminent. The BBC reported that the killings were escalating, the rival armies were becoming more active daily and the Foreign Office was advising everyone to leave Mogadishu. It seemed that civil war was about to engulf the city. We held a meeting and decided the time had come to leave. We had our own personal weapons and some ammunition, but we knew we didn't have enough to take on much more than 20 or so trained Somali soldiers. And none of us had any wish to end up dead, lying on a sun-baked dirt road in Somalia with gaping wounds and 1,000 flies buzzing around our rotting bodies.

'Let's get out while we can,' someone said.

Dave, who was still in command, asked everyone, 'Anyone against that plan?'

We all shook our heads. 'Let's go while we still can,' someone said. 'I would hate to be trapped here if the fighting really took a hold.'

Dave and myself went to see the businessmen and told them that they should seriously consider our advice and leave the city before the shit hit the fan. We also told them that the situation had deteriorated to such a degree that we could no longer guarantee their safety. They understood and decided they, too, would quit while still alive. Although we had been in Somalia for something over five weeks, we had received four weeks' pay in advance but no money had been offered for the fifth week. We wondered if there would be any further payments. In the circumstances, that seemed fair. No one argued, but we would have all liked the extra week's pay owed to us. We thought we had deserved it.

The drive to the airport and the flight back to Britain went without a hitch. No one tried to stop us after leaving the hotel and making our way in the vehicles to Mogadishu Airport. But we were all very relieved once we had taken off and headed home. I could see the relief on everyone's faces, thankful that we had all escaped, except for the unfortunate American who had bought it in the accident. In fact, we were so happy to be out of the place that we all became seriously drunk on the flight back. So drunk, in fact, that the cabin staff ended up refusing to serve us any more drinks because we were all completely legless. Most of us spent the final hour of the flight sleeping it off. And it was great to land at Heathrow and realise that we were back in civilisation.

There was only one aspect we found galling. We never knew who, in fact, had employed us. Our pay had been given to us in cash, most of it before leaving the UK, when we all met prior to flying out of Heathrow. On our return to Britain, we tried to discover who had employed us, promising the world but not exactly delivering. Every contact we telephoned and tried to trace didn't seem to exist. Whenever we tried our contact phone numbers, the person answering advised us to ring another number because they could not help. They were all polite but adamant that they knew nothing which could help us trace our employers. After a few days of being given the bum's rush, we called it a day. It had been one adventure I had no wish to repeat. I vowed to keep out of any further trouble, but that seemed an impossibility — worse, much worse, would follow.

CHAPTER ELEVEN

The steel cell door clanged shut behind me. I looked around at the tiny cell, the tiny window, the steel bed, the table and chair and the daunting, reinforced, blue steel door that had just shut me in, cutting me off from the rest of the world. As I heard the footsteps of the prison warder disappearing into silence, I felt suddenly alone and a fear of the unknown gripped me. I had survived gun battles in the Middle East and dangerous assignments tackling armed drug gangs, and had never felt a moment's fear, but now I was totally alone, without a friend or companion, and the feeling unnerved me.

As though in a daze I examined my cell in more detail. There was a single chair and a small table, both made from cardboard. The steel bed, with slats instead of springs, was bolted to the concrete floor; the stainless steel lavatory in the corner could only be operated by a push button and the bars on the tiny window were so thick and so close together it was virtually impossible to see the world outside.

I stood by the door and took in my new surroundings shaking my head slowly, wondering what the hell had happened to land me in solitary confinement in a British jail. Worse still was the fact that I was being treated as a highly dangerous prisoner. My heart sank to my boots and I tried to clear my head, to help me work out how the hell I was going to get out of this appalling fucking mess.

'Fuck me,' I thought, 'I wouldn't mind if I had done something to deserve all this but I've done nothing wrong, absolutely nothing. I am completely and totally innocent.' I knew that I had done nothing wrong. I had broken no law. I just happened to be in the wrong fucking place at the wrong fucking time. For that sin, for that moment of bad luck, I was being treated as a desperate and highly dangerous prisoner.

It seemed all wrong. For seven years I had served Queen and Country as a loyal and keen member of the armed forces. I had obeyed the rules and had given of my best to become what I hoped had been a credit to the Royal Marines and the Special Boat Service. I had felt privileged to be a member of both units. I had been fortunate in getting to know a great bunch of lads for whom I would have risked my neck to save in an emergency if ever the occasion arose. And I had total trust in them. I believed that being a member of the SBS was an honour not to be taken lightly and though the going was often extremely arduous, tough and nerve-racking, there was a feeling that being a part of the SBS was something that had been earned the hard way and was a noble, right-minded organisation whose motives were above suspicion and whose dedication was incomparable.

Despite all that, here I was in one of Her Majesty's top-security prisons, in fucking solitary confinement and being treated like some son-of-a-bitch, poxy gunman running drugs shipments into Britain. It seemed absolutely fucking preposterous. But here I was and God alone knew how the hell I was going to get out of this tight spot.

Officially, I had been designated a high-risk Category 'A' prisoner by the Home Office. According to the Prison Officer whom I got to know chatting through my blue steel door, I had been categorised as the eighth most dangerous man in Britain. I couldn't believe what I was hearing; I couldn't understand why the authorities would want to believe the very worst, condemning me with not a shred of evidence, taking not the slightest notice of what I had to say, refusing to listen to my explanation and then treating me like a fucking convict. I had served in Northern Ireland and I knew the way convicted Provo gunmen and bombers were treated over there. And here was I slammed up in solitary with no previous convictions; I'd made no attempt to resist arrest; I had an impeccable service record and no criminal record at all; there had been no evidence against me and I hadn't been charged with any offence whatsoever; and here I was, being treated far worse than Provos and Loyalists convicted of murder and bombings.

Over and over again, I mulled over

everything that had gone wrong. Shit, I had fuck all else to do all day and half the night. And the more I thought of the way I was being treated, like some fucking dangerous animal, the more angry and frustrated I became. The whole thing was ridiculous and if it hadn't been so bloody serious I would have laughed at what had happened to me. But this was serious. I kept thinking: 'If they're treating me like this when I've done nothing wrong, how the fuck will they treat me if I am convicted of some trumped-up charge?'

For the first seven days of my solitary confinement, I was left to sweat it out in that abominable cell. For some extraordinary reason, the Prison authorities refused to permit me to wash or shower, refused to let me shave or brush my teeth for the first few days, refused to let me out of my cell on any pretext whatsoever. I was not permitted to visit the exercise yard nor was any lawyer permitted to see me or talk to me. At the end of those seven days I was literally in a stinking state and I wondered what the hell was going to happen next. I knew it was utterly scandalous the way I was being treated but there was nothing, absolutely fuck-all, that I could do.

All that made me feel angry, too, and usually I'm a quiet, happy-go-lucky sort of bloke. But in that fucking cell I was fuming with rage and frustration.

I would sit on the floor, my back against the wall, my legs sticking out across the cell, my head deep in my chest, wondering when something would break, when someone would be permitted to see me. For all I knew there was no one out there who had any idea where I was or what I was doing. I had not been permitted to telephone anyone, not even my parents, my girlfriend or a mate, and certainly not a lawyer.

Time and again I asked my screw to request that I should be allowed to phone a lawyer or ask a lawyer to represent me. Time and again I asked to be allowed to phone my parents, to tell them what had happened and explain that I had done nothing wrong. I asked that I be allowed to phone my darling girlfriend, to put her mind at rest, but the answer was always the same: 'Sorry, mate, the answer's no.'

At the end of that week, my Prison Officer finally took pity on me. He could see the physical state I was in. I was filthy and smelly. I felt disgusted with myself but I could do fuck-all about it. I thought it was outrageous that anyone should be treated in this way. This was Britain in the 1990s, a country proud of its judicial system, where a man is allegedly innocent until proven guilty. I was being treated worse than a convicted prisoner in a third-world country, banged up in solitary and not even permitted to wash, shave, shower or clean my teeth. It seemed that the authorities couldn't care less. Every day, I asked the duty prison officers to allow me to wash, shave and shower. Every time they refused my request, saying they were simply obeying orders.

I realised, thank God, the game they were playing, treating me in such a disgusting fashion. They were obviously trying to break my spirit, hoping that I would confess to whatever they wanted by making me feel like some sub-human species, banged up 24 hours a day and living in disgusting conditions. Throughout those days, I barely ate anything served up to me, but only drank the water. I was worried in case they 'spiked' the food in some way, because it would have been so easy to do so while I was in solitary. I was not thinking straight. I knew it wasn't the prison officers' fault, but still couldn't understand how badly I was treated. I had heard stories of additives being concealed in food offered to prisoners to affect their brains. I believed that if they were deliberately keeping me in such squalid, filthy conditions, then they were likely to take any liberties they wanted with me. In that first week, I must have lost 5kg in weight.

After several days, one officer agreed to telephone my parents to tell them that I was alive and well and in good health, but that I had not been in contact with them because I was being held in solitary confinement at Horfield High Security Prison in Bristol. I asked them to get me a lawyer. I did not want to tell them the conditions in which I was being held, because the last thing I wanted to do was upset my mother. I knew she would be extremely worried at the mere fact that I was in jail. If I had told her the details, she would have immediately driven to the jail and confronted the Governor. And I didn't think that would be diplomatic!

My lawyer finally persuaded the Prison authorities and the Home Office that he had every right to see his client and he was permitted to visit me. I shall never forget the look on his face when he stood in front of me, his mouth open, his eyes hardly able to take in the fact that I was his client, a bearded, dishevelled, unwashed, stinking hulk of a man.

He went ballistic.

He turned to the Duty Prison Officer and told him, 'This man is being treated worse than a dog. How dare you keep a man in solitary in this condition? It's outrageous.'

'Just following orders, Sir,' came the pathetic reply.

'Well, if you do not permit my client to shower, wash and shave this instant, then I will raise this matter with the highest authority.'

'We were only ...' began the Prison Officer.

But my lawyer had no wish to hear his reply. He interrupted, 'I've heard what you said but this is absolutely disgraceful. My client has been convicted of no crime, and yet you are treating him like some wild animal. Now listen to what I'm saying. This man must be permitted to wash, shave and shower, and be given a fresh set of clothes, immediately. Do you understand me?'

'Yes, Sir,' came the reply.

'Well, do whatever you have to do,' my lawyer replied. 'Take advice if necessary. But I have no intention of leaving here until those demands are met. Is that understood?'

'Yes, Sir,' came the reply.

That first shower was utter bliss. It was absolutely wonderful to stand under that shower with hot water pouring over my body. I cleaned and washed and scrubbed myself, washing my hair three times. I could have stayed in that shower for an hour, but the authorities wouldn't permit that. In any case, I had to get out and see my lawyer who had been waiting for me. I shaved, gently and painfully, and put on clean clothes. When I walked in to see my lawyer, I felt like a new man.

Then I told him what had happened and why I had found myself branded a Category 'A' prisoner in a high-security British jail. At first, I wasn't sure he believed me, but as the details of the case unfolded and the circumstances leading up to my arrest on the high seas became more apparent, he became convinced that I was indeed totally innocent of any criminal offence. It had just been sheer bad luck.

I wondered in those days and weeks and months that I lived out my life in the horror of solitary confinement, whether I had just been a bloody fool who had ignored common sense or simply had been too trusting. Whatever the reason, I had been well and truly stuffed.

I had returned from the heat and sweat of the hell-hole that was Somalia in 1996 and decided to lead a quiet life back in the UK. I found a job renovating the original stone floors of old cottages and listed buildings near the beautiful, peaceful village of Castle Coombe in Wiltshire, which must be one of the most picturesque places in Britain. It was good, hard, solid work earning me £300 a week. Life was great.

I was living with my beautiful girlfriend, Clare, a 5ft 6in tall blonde, with a great body, whom I had known since my days in the SBS. She was a superbly fit, athletic young woman who was great fun as well as being straight, honest and trustworthy. I knew I had a great girlfriend because all my mates called me a 'lucky bastard' living with such a lovely girl. We shared a flat in Bristol and spent our weekdays working hard and our weekends in bed together. It was life at its best.

Out of the blue, I received a phonecall from Don, an old SBS mate who was still serving with the Royal Marines.

'Someone I know is looking for a diving instructor to take charge of a professional diving school in Spain, a few miles outside Barcelona,' he said. 'I wondered if you might be interested?'

Without thinking, I asked Don who was behind the venture and whether the school had been properly kitted out with all the necessary equipment. I had heard of other diving schools that had been started with a pair of flippers and a snorkel and I wanted nothing to do with such cowboy outfits.

'This one's genuine,' Don replied. 'I wouldn't have suggested the idea to you if it hadn't been a proper outfit. The owners want a top-class instructor and I thought you might be interested.'

'I'm not sure,' I replied, 'I'll have to think about it. I've got a good job and a great girl I'm living with at the moment.'

'Listen,' replied Don, 'why don't you come out here for a couple of weeks and inspect the outfit. Bring your girl with you; take a holiday. I'm sure they would pay your air fares and you could stay there for nothing. I can fix that.'

That sounded a great idea. We could go out there, enjoy a holiday in the sun and check out the school. It was December and cold at home and the idea of a bit of winter sun sounded attractive. We could spend Christmas and New Year at home together and then piss off to Spain.

'You're on,' I said. 'I'll have to fix things this end and Clare will have to take a couple of weeks' holiday. Hopefully, we'll see you in a couple of weeks but I'll let you know the dates in a few days. How's that?'

'Magic,' said Don. 'I'm sure you'll love the place. I'll be seeing you then. Call me.'

Six weeks later, Clare and I flew out of freezing Britain to the warm winter sun of Barcelona. We had open minds about whether I should take the job or not. At least we would have a great holiday together. As we joked on the flight out, we might not have much sun and sea at that time of year, but we intended to enjoy everything else. And we did.

We were met by Don and together we checked out the diving school which was situated 20 miles north of Barcelona in a typically romantic Spanish fishing village which had, unfortunately, been taken over by the tourist industry 20 years earlier. At this time of year, however, the village had been reclaimed by the Spanish families who lived in the surrounding countryside and they were generous and hospitable. They made us feel at home and they loved Clare.

The diving school was being run by an intelligent 30-year-old Spaniard called Pedro who had been in the Spanish Marines. He spoke fluent English, and he knew his stuff. He was obviously a very competent diver and we got on famously. He explained that although he could speak English well, those people who had invested in the well-equipped outfit wanted an Englishman to bring in the tourists. They believed that having a former SBS Royal Marine as Chief Instructor gave the school credibility and the tourists would trust that the venture was a well-run, professional outfit. I was hooked. I fancied spending my summer months in Spain enjoying the sun and the warm sea, the holiday atmosphere and the job of a diving instructor running my own show.

Three weeks after moving out to Spain, I met Paul, a young 30-something London property developer who had moved out to Spain intent on building villas which he would either rent out or sell to Brits wanting to settle in the country. He lived in a beautiful, huge, white-painted Spanish villa with his wife and two young children. Their villa had six bedrooms, three bathrooms, a huge patio, a large inviting swimming pool and the whole place was surrounded by a luscious green garden and hidden from sight by palm trees stretching down to the 6ft-high perimeter wall.

To me, it seemed that Paul and his family were living in paradise. I decided I wanted a piece of the action, though nothing so grand or expensive. In my dreams, I saw myself running a diving school and living in a secluded Spanish cottage with a swimming pool and patio and, most important of all, with Clare.

Clare had to fly home. I became good friends with Paul and when his wife and kids went off to Britain for a few weeks at a time, we became great drinking mates. He gave me the run of the villa with my own suite of rooms and I moved in. But I missed Clare terribly. So Clare would work a non-stop shift for ten days and then fly out to Barcelona for five days with me. The flight cost me only £30 for most of the year and we would live together in Paul's magnificent home. Then she would fly off again, returning ten or eleven days later. It worked really well and we got on famously together.

The more I talked to Paul about my ambitions and aspirations, the more he was happy to help and encourage me. He told me that if I came up with a good, sensible business venture he would happily back it, if he believed there was a chance of success. One day, we discussed the idea of buying an old vessel and running a diving school from it. The plan was to purchase a suitable boat for me to covert to a floating diving school with cabins and bunk beds, a good-sized dining area and modern galley. I would be the diving instructor and we would employ someone to skipper the boat and hire a crew. Through advertisements in the travel pages of British newspapers, we would offer all-inclusive holidays, with bed, board, food, lodging, wine and beer, for an all-in price of £400 per person per week. We wanted a boat which could comfortably accommodate 20 paying passengers and the crew. Included in that £400 figure was the diving instruction. We aimed to train a novice to a competent level during a one-week course. And Paul and I would split the profits.

I found an old 1966 Dutch trawler, approximately 35 metres long and capable of sleeping 30 people, in an English ships-for-sale publication. The trawler, purchased through a shipping agent, cost £30,000. We hired a mate of mine, Jim, as skipper and recruited a crew of five Spanish seamen and a Turk. Then we began advertising the diving holidays through British travel agents. We also had 500 leaflets printed which we left in diving schools wherever we touched land.

We collected the vessel from Malta and during the following few weeks visited the Balearic islands in the Mediterranean, Tunis, Gibraltar, Portugal and Gran Canaria. There proved to be a hell of a lot of work that needed to be done to make the ship comfortable as well as presentable to holidaymakers wanting to enjoy a rest as well as learning to dive. Most of those weeks were spent repairing the boat and working on the engines which kept breaking down. I spent many hours welding, cutting and stripping out the cabins — in other words, undertaking a major re-fit.

I also had some fun. When the sun was hot and high the dolphins would swim alongside the vessel and I would watch them until I became so desperate for a swim I would simply leap over the side, shouting to my mates, 'Man overboard.' I would land among the dolphins and we would swim along together. My mate Jim, the skipper, was not at all happy with me for it meant he had to slow the vessel and then turn completely around to come and pick me up again. This would take perhaps 20 minutes, and in the meantime I would be playing and swimming with the dolphins, having great fun. They were curious, swimming close to me and then darting away while others would stay away and then dart suddenly towards me, checking me out. They are truly amazing and seem so intelligent.

The first time I did this Jim thought it was amusing, but by the sixth time he was downright annoyed with me. But I wanted to swim with the dolphins so much I took the risk of upsetting him.

On one occasion, a shoal of turtles swam close to the ship; that was too tempting so I dived in once more with my customary, 'Man overboard.' The turtles treated me with more disdain than the dolphins, keeping their distance. But they didn't swim away, allowing me to swim along with them as long as I didn't try to get too close. By and large, Jim took my antics in good heart, but I realised I had become a damn nuisance so I stopped fooling around. Most of the day, I wore nothing but a pair of boxer shorts and flip-flops and made sure I got a really good tan. Usually, the temperature was around 80° Fahrenheit, sometimes even too hot to sunbathe.

While cruising steadily at about eight knots an hour about 40 miles off the coast of Morocco, the ship's engines died. We were lying dead in the water with no power whatsoever. It meant days of trying to get the problem sorted and then hoping the vessel would stagger as far as Gibraltar for a major engine overhaul. We eventually made it to Gibraltar where the engine was sorted and we took off once more, visiting various locations and establishing links with travel organisations around the Mediterranean in an effort to boost the business that I hoped would give me a well-paid, interesting job for at least six months a year. Though many of my mates who had served with the Royal Marines were happy to become more closely involved in the security business, acting as bodyguards and mercenaries, risking their necks in African adventures, my experience in Somalia had cured me of any romantic notions of earning my living as a soldier of fortune in God-forsaken countries around the globe. I wanted something that I could control and enjoy, like running my very own diving school and happily tootling around the Med, teaching people how to become competent underwater divers.

Except for the ship's engines which seemed to be constantly in need of repair, life was great. I enjoyed the hard work of re-fitting the vessel as we chugged merrily around the Mediterranean, enjoying the few days in port, relaxing with a few beers in some romantic location and enjoying the sun that, in May 1997, was shining out of bright, blue cloudless skies. Life was idyllic and I was in my element. All I wanted now was for the holiday season to begin in earnest and enough people to want to learn to dive and enjoy a week on board our spruced-up, old Dutch trawler.

As I lay on my bunk in my own cabin, I drifted off to sleep with the chug-chug-chug of the engines reminding me that all was well in the world. Suddenly, I awoke and there was silence. The engines had stopped. 'Shit,' I thought, 'I don't fuckin' believe it. Not again.'

The engines were my responsibility because I was the one person on board who had undergone an engineering course in the Royal Marines and was fairly competent in looking after most problems. I swung out of my bunk, pulled on a pair of shorts and walked out of my cabin, intending to ask the officer on watch what had happened before venturing down into the bowels of the ship to see if I could repair whatever had gone wrong.

I went up on deck and saw a fishing boat next to our vessel and a band of a dozen men hauling great bundles of stuffed sacks on to the port side of our boat.

'What the fuck's going on?' I asked someone, trying to come to terms with what I saw. He didn't reply but just continued unloading the sacks from the fishing boat to our vessel.

Like a bolt of lightning, I suddenly realised what was happening. I had seen large 25kg sacks just like these while with the SBS and they were always filled with the same merchandise — cannabis. These were the same type of sacking that I had seen and examined when we had been carrying out drug-busting operations for HM Customs and Excise.

My heart sank. In that instant, I realised all my dreams were over, my ambitions shattered, my thoughts of running a diving school gone in a flash. I had believed I was part of a new business venture in which I was to be a major player. Now I realised I had been fucking conned. It had all been a fucking sham, a charade. There never was going to be a diving school. I had simply been encouraged to re-fit this old trawler, keep the engines going and swan around the Mediterranean as a cover for a drug-smuggling operation.

I cursed myself and felt angry and disillusioned. What a stupid, great, fucking idiot I had been. What a fool I was to have been taken in like this and not to have realised what was going to happen. I had thought that all the sailing around the Mediterranean and the Atlantic was for a purpose, visiting ports and resorts here and there, spreading the word of our new diving vessel. In reality, it was obvious the voyage was intended to confuse the anti-drugs authorities who might have thought we were suspicious and had decided to track our movements.

Suddenly, everything made sense. The

decrepit old ship bought through an agent, collected in Malta and then repaired in various ports; the pantomime of the diving school venture; the extraordinary smoke-screen itinerary, criss-crossing the shipping lanes, lying low for days in various ports. I presumed that this all had been meticulously planned to ensure that any Customs authorities, who might have had suspicions as to the real motives behind the Dutch trawler, would have lost interest.

'Who's in charge?' I asked, and was told to talk to the Spanish skipper of the Moroccan fishing boat who fortunately could speak English.

'What's going on?' I asked him.

'Are you Mercer?' he asked. 'Peter Mercer?'

'Yes,' I replied.

'I have a question for you,' he replied.

'What's that?' I asked.

'If you want, you are invited to join our syndicate,' he explained. 'You can do so. This shipment is being transported to Holland. If you want to join us you will receive £200,000 after the delivery is made. But you will have to tell no one, of course. What do you think?'

'I want nothing whatsoever to do with any of

this,' I told him. 'I want nothing to do with drugs, nothing at all.'

'What do you want to do then?' he asked.

'Where are you going with this fishing boat?' I asked.

'We are returning to Morocco, of course,' he replied.

'Good,' I replied, 'I'll come with you. I don't want to stay on this boat another minute. I want out.'

'But you can't,' replied the skipper, 'you can't come with us.'

'Why not?' I persisted. 'I want to get off this boat now and you can take me to Morocco.'

I went to my cabin, threw all my belongings into a bag and went back on deck, intending to get into the fishing boat and fly back to England from Morocco.

I said farewell to Jim, but the parting wasn't very friendly because I was convinced in my heart that he must have known something about the plans before we had even purchased the trawler. But I was prepared to give him the benefit of the doubt, because I knew that he was receiving his orders and headings from on-shore throughout our voyage. He had no idea from one day to the next where we were going, but he would obey orders from the owners.

I threw my gear on to the fishing smack and went to clamber aboard. But as I did so, someone threw my bag back on to the deck of our vessel.

'What are you doing that for?' I asked. 'I'm coming with you.'

'You can't come with us,' said the Skipper. 'I told you no.'

'Why not?' I asked.

'When we were on our way to this rendezvous with you, we were intercepted by a rival gang. They had guns and they fired at us trying to make us stop, so they could come on board and take all the sacks,' he said.

'They were firing at you?' I asked. 'Was anyone injured? Did the attack cause any damage?'

'That does not matter,' he explained. 'But there will be trouble on the way back and we don't want you in the middle of trouble. They might think you are the man behind all this and target you. You cannot come with us.'

I was worried, and feared what was going to happen. I had been on the other side on many occasions, raiding boats suspected of carrying drugs. I knew what the SBS are like in those circumstances. They are tough and deliberately put the fear of God into everyone on board when they raid a ship. It's no picnic.

But I was in a no-win situation. If the Moroccans refused to take me with them, then I had no alternative but to sit it out and get off the fucking boat at the earliest possible opportunity. I also knew that until my feet touched land, I would be a very worried man, searching the skies every day and checking the horizon in case the SBS were on their way in their RIBs. I also knew that 5.00am was the time to remain alert and check the skies in case they decided to parachute the SBS teams and the RIBs from a Hercules 130 in a dawn raid.

Suddenly, I pulled myself back to the present. It was time for thought and action, not for worrying about the future. I realised that the bulging 25 kilo sacks on the deck were an open invitation to anyone searching for drug smugglers to order the authorities to intercept and search the boat. So I ordered the crew to stuff the sacks into the hold as quickly as possible and to make damned sure not a single sack was left in view of any prying eyes.

I picked up my bag and walked back to my cabin, feeling sick in my stomach at what could happen. But as I lay on my bunk, I wondered for a moment or so whether I had been too hasty; I wondered whether I should have gone along with the deal; taken the £200,000 on offer and, if caught, done the nine months in a cushy Dutch jail. But as quickly as the thought crossed my mind, I realised that I couldn't live with that on my mind, nor would I ever again be able to look my parents in the eye. Going along with the gang would have made me rich but also a deeply, miserable man. I didn't want to know.

The following day I spoke to Jim and asked him where we were going. He told me he had been given headings taking us around the tip of Scotland and then into the North Sea, to the Hook of Holland, keeping clear of the Norwegian coast, making sure we remained in international waters. He believed the voyage would take a minimum of two weeks. It was going to be a long and anxious 14 days.

And then the engine broke down.

That's all we needed. I was now convinced that we would be caught with this mountain of cannabis on board and God knows what would happen. I kept wondering how I would be able to convince Customs and the police that I was entirely innocent and knew nothing whatsoever about the drug-smuggling plot. The more I thought about my precarious situation the more I realised I was absolutely and completely in the shit. Rather than believe me, they would just laugh in my face and insist that I stop telling porkies.

I knew the old engine — an American Lister tank engine — wasn't to blame, and I suspected the red diesel we used or the fuel supply lines which always seemed to be clogging. I serviced the engine yet again, cleaned the filters and checked the fuel injection system. We had two generators on board, a 220-volt which had blown, and a 110-volt. The 220 ran the all-important refrigerator, TV and the lighting system, and it was impossible for me to repair. We would have to call for assistance or risk checking into a port that was capable of repairing it. I told Jim that it would be impossible to make the trip to the Hook of Holland because we wouldn't have enough food to survive on. I calculated that, within 48 hours, all the perishable food and drinks would have gone off.

Shattered after a day of hard work, struggling to repair the generator and checking the engine and fuel supply system, I turned in shortly after 9pm. I put the Walkman to my ears and listened to one of my all-time favourite tunes, 'The Fun Loving Criminals', while I glanced at a motorbike magazine. Some time later I drifted off to sleep.

For some unknown reason I awoke shortly after midnight and drowsily turned off my Walkman and the bedside light. I lay down again and closed my eyes. Towards the very back of my mind I thought I heard someone counting, a man's voice saying, 'One … two … three.'

That was it. In that split second my brain leapt into action, recalling that this was the SBS countdown procedure, the entry count, whispered so only those in the bust could hear. I knew what was coming next, I knew what to expect.

I slammed my hands over my ears and shut my eyes tightly as the explosion reverberated around my tiny cabin, the flash of the charge infiltrating my closed eyes. Then I heard an almighty crash as the wooden door splintered, and the stun-grenade exploded in the cabin. I knew what effect those grenades had on unsuspecting people, particularly in such small, confined spaces. I had witnessed them; I had used them myself in similar missions. The flash temporarily blinds and disorientates the occupants, and the noise numbs the senses. The victim is left in a state of total shock for a matter of seconds, long enough for an entry team to smash their way into a room and take command of the place before the shock has worn off. Stun-grenades are an incredibly effective weapon in such circumstances and yet they don't cause any injury.

After the explosion and the flashes, I opened my eyes as the team of three — all dressed in black protective clothing and balaclavas — came bursting through the door, screaming orders.

'Get on the floor, get on the floor now,' they yelled.

I knew the drill by heart, and yet I still felt scared at the speed and severity of their behaviour when arresting me. Two held Heckler

& Koch MP5s to my head, their fingers on the triggers, while the third threw me to the floor, grabbed the hair at the back of my head and forcefully pushed my face to the floorboards. He pulled my hands behind my back and cable-tied them, the cables biting into my wrists. I was naked and felt totally vulnerable. I knew, from my own experience, that the victim usually receives a few hard kicks if he doesn't move fast enough or stay perfectly still. It's done to put the victim at a disadvantage, to make him feel vulnerable and useless, to make him realise there is no point whatsoever in putting up an argument or a fight. And now I had first-hand knowledge why very few ever tried to argue or escape.

As I lay motionless on the floor, I heard other stun-grenades going off at the entrance to other cabins, and the voices of mates whom I thought I recognised, barking orders at the terrified victims who had been fast asleep when the SBS launched their midnight raid. I also realised what a desperate situation I was in, arrested on the high seas with tons of fucking cannabis on board and no excuse.

'Are there any guns on board?' one of my

former SBS mates asked me.

'No, none,' I replied. 'Well, I haven't seen any. I don't think there are any on board.'

'Are you sure, Pete?' one asked.

'Pretty sure,' I replied.

'Good,' he said, 'now keep still. You know the drill.'

'OK,' I replied.

The last thing I was going to do was attempt to escape or try anything stupid, which might be construed as suspicious. Somehow, I had to prove my innocence but I hadn't the foggiest idea how I was going to do that.

After five minutes or so, after more explosions and the noise of SBS men screaming orders at their terrified victims, a silence suddenly descended on the boat. I could still hear people running about and the odd shouted order, but there was a sudden calm about the place. I lay still, not daring to move a muscle, because the last thing I wanted to do was give the lads the wrong impression. Already, they must have known the boat was full of tons of cannabis and, understandably, believed that I was part of the drug-smuggling gang. I had been out of the SBS for a couple of months and they must have thought the worst of me. I couldn't blame them. All the evidence showed that I was well and truly in the frame.

Then a man from HM Customs walked into the cabin, but of course I couldn't see him. 'Do you speak English?' he asked.

'Yes,' I replied.

He bent down and pushed a card in my face. 'Read this,' he said. It was his HM Customs ID card.

'You know you're in the shit, don't you?' he asked.

''Course I do,' I replied.

After asking my name which, of course, I gave him, he told me that I was under arrest on suspicion of smuggling Category B drugs into the United Kingdom. I said nothing in reply. There was nothing I could say at that moment. I knew it was useless to discuss the matter with the arresting officer. My explanation would have to wait until I reached land. There, I would hopefully find a lawyer who would believe my story. I'd tell him everything and hope that he would be able to prove my innocence and save my skin. But in my heart I knew the odds were stacked against me.

Twenty minutes later, one of the SBS team came into my cabin and cut the cable ties from my wrists. My hands had turned blue during that time as the cables had been so tightly pulled together. I rubbed my wrists to get the blood back into my hands.

'Right, get dressed,' he said, 'and don't try any funny business.'

'Don't worry, I won't,' I replied.

There was no way I was going to try anything with the Marine holding an MP5 which he was pointing straight at me. I dressed in jeans, a sweat-shirt and flip-flops.

'Let's go,' he said and I was told to walk in front of him with my hands behind my back. On deck, a life-jacket was put on me and I tied the strings, and I was told to get into the RIB. My former SBS mates were on deck, their MP5s at the ready, as I made my way along the deck to the RIB.

The one-mile ride from the trawler to HMS York, which was to take us into port, was choppy that morning and we were bumped around all over the place as the RIB cut through the water at speed.

Before attempting to climb the Jacob's

ladder to the deck of HMS York someone shouted, 'Don't fall in, Pete.'

I gave him an old-fashioned look and climbed the ladder. On deck were three sailors, who we always called matelots in the Marines, holding their SA80 firearms, their muzzles pointing directly at us as we clambered aboard. I looked at them, somewhat concerned. They appeared highly nervous, which worried me. There is a saying in the Marines — 'There's only one thing more dangerous than an officer with a map; that's a matelot with a gun.'

As Jim came aboard behind me, he whispered, 'I hope one of them doesn't open fire, he'll kill the lot of us.'

Jim, who was a well-built, athletic man, about 6ft 2in tall, turned to one of the sailors and told him, 'What the fuck are you pointing that gun at me for, it's not even cocked!'

'Don't try anything,' replied the matelot.

'If you don't get that fucking thing out of my face,' Jim said menacingly, 'I'll grab it off you and stick it up your arse. Get it?'

The matelots looked at each other and meekly took their guns away from our faces. Then the Chief Petty Officer came up with cable-ties and put them on our wrists. I looked down at mine. He had fastened them incorrectly, so that by simply twisting the wrist the cable handcuffs would fall off. I looked at Jim, winked and looked down at my handcuffs. Then I slipped them off and handed them to the Chief Petty Officer.

'Excuse me, mate,' I said, 'you've put these on the wrong way.'

He looked daggers at me and re-fastened them, this time making sure they were secure. In court some months later, HM Customs claimed that this had been an 'escape attempt' on my part and, as a result, they were against me being granted bail. All I had done was inform the Officer that my cuffs had been put on wrongly. And there was another point which was not mentioned in court. What chance would I have had to escape when we were on a Royal Navy warship, under armed guard, in the middle of the ocean some hundreds of miles from Britain?

We were taken below decks, strip-searched and given fresh clothes. Our own clothes were apparently required as evidence in a probable forthcoming trial. For most of the three-day trip back to England, Jim was locked in the paint cupboard and I was put in a tiny lavatory. The only place to sit down was on the toilet. And there was just space to stand up, but it was impossible to lie down in that cramped space. Food was brought and handed to me, but I didn't touch anything. I feared the food and drink could have been 'spiked' by some smart-arse in the galley, so I only drank water the entire time we were locked up.

After we had docked at Plymouth, we were manacled and led up on deck. Standing there were about 20 matelots armed with SA80s and pick-handles. Lined up on the jetty were four police cars with 25 cops standing in line, all armed with MP5s and Sig 226 automatics. It was obvious they were taking no chances with this drug-smuggling gang of Jim, me, five Spaniards and a Turk.

As we walked off the warship, Jim couldn't suppress one last piss-taking remark: 'Thanks for having us, lads,' he said, 'nice ride.'

No one replied.

Still cuffed, we were put in the police cars and driven the five miles to Charles Cross Station at breakneck speed, the sirens blaring, outriders stopping on-coming traffic. In front was a Land Rover Discovery with armed police inside and another at the rear of the convoy.

On arrival at the station, we were led in and after giving our names, addresses, ages and occupations, we were formally charged with conspiracy to import cannabis resin to the UK. Then we were put in a cell and offered a mug of tea.

I asked if I could clean my teeth, as I hadn't been permitted any such luxuries while on board HMS York. 'No,' came the reply, 'you're SBS. We've heard of your tricks. You could make explosives out of the toothpaste and blast your way out of this jail.'

I was amazed at such a stupid idea. 'You've seen too many James Bond films,' I said, and left it at that.

Then I was allowed to see a lawyer, provided by the police. I asked him what advice he would give me.

'Say nothing,' he said, 'don't answer any questions, whatever they ask you or say to you. To every question simply reply "no comment". Don't tell them anything about yourself, your family, your career, your job, nothing. Got it?'

'Got it,' I replied.

Then I heard I was to be transferred to

Horfield High Security prison in Bristol. That trip made me smile. I couldn't stop myself. I very nearly burst out laughing. To escort me to Horfield, the police laid on a helicopter which flew over the convoy throughout the entire journey; six police outriders, two Land Rover Discoveries with armed police inside, a riot van with more armed police and four cars.

On arrival at Horfield, I was put in 'G' Wing, reserved for the most dangerous prisoners. After that first horrific week alone in my cell, not permitted to wash, shave, shower or change my clothes, I felt I would be able to face anything. But life inside would still turn out to be tough, bloody tough.

I was banged up 23 hours a day, and only permitted one hour's exercise daily, and that was in a tiny yard with steel mesh, 10ft above the ground, covering the top. Even then I was only permitted to exercise on my own. There were never any other prisoners there, only two guards with dogs keeping an eye on me. I was allowed no visitors without Home Office approval, nor permitted to make any telephone calls until security clearance had been given by the Prison Governor and the Home Office.

But I was allowed to write letters, read six books a week and eventually to make telephone calls. It was fantastic to talk to Clare and my parents on the phone. Of course, I tried to reassure them that I was not guilty of any criminal activity and certainly not guilty of drug smuggling. Clare was fantastic, standing by me throughout the months I was in jail, which must have been very difficult for her. I knew that some people would have inevitably been suspicious, suggesting that there was 'no smoke without fire' and suspecting that I must have known there were tons of cannabis on board. But I forgave anyone who harboured those thoughts, because they didn't know all the circumstances.

I was longing to see Clare and my parents, to tell them what had happened in some detail so that they would understand how I had found myself in solitary confinement in a maximum-security jail and treated like a dangerous criminal. Finally, after three weeks, Clare was given permission to visit me. After hearing that piece of news, I could hardly contain my excitement. Without doubt, those first three weeks were the most unbearable and distressing weeks of my entire life. Sometimes, I feared that I would never walk out of that jail alive; at other times, I wondered whether I would ever see Clare or my parents again.

The night before she visited me, I didn't sleep a wink, waiting anxiously to see her, fearing that she might not come and trying not to build up my hopes too much in case something happened and she was unable to make the trip. I also feared that the prison authorities might have been playing games with me, suddenly withdrawing permission for the visit at the last minute by making some pathetic excuse and calling off the meeting.

As I was escorted to the visitor's wing — reserved for Category 'A' prisoners only — I was physically shaking at the prospect of actually seeing Clare again. The precautions undertaken that day by the prison authorities were unbelievable. I was handcuffed to two prison officers while a third walked in front of me. Before I was even allowed into the courtyard leading to the visitors' wing, every other prisoner had to withdraw and go to their cells. In the courtyard leading from G Wing, three more officers, with Alsatians, stood guard. I was strip-searched twice, once before leaving my cell, the second time in the visitor's wing. And before being allowed to see Clare, I had to change my clothes entirely, dressing in 'sterile' clothing. I would have to change again after the meeting and undergo further strip-searches. And what was so extraordinary was the fact that throughout the time I saw Clare, we were never permitted to kiss or touch each other because there was a glass screen dividing us in the tiny room, which only measured 7ft by 4ft. And throughout the meeting, four prison officers stood just a few feet behind me the entire time.

Clare was in tears, distressed at my appearance and naturally upset by everything she had heard. She broke down when I told her that my lawyer had warned me that the case might take two years before coming to court. And I didn't blame her. She had her whole life before her and here was I, her boyfriend who loved her, banged up in solitary. I tried to reassure her, but it was so difficult with plate-glass between us and four officers standing only a couple of feet behind me; our conversation was awkward and embarrassing. Much of the time we simply looked at each other, and I tried in a small way to reassure her of my innocence. But it was a nerve-racking, heart-rending meeting. It frustrated me because I had no idea how long it would be before I would be out of the jail and able to talk to her privately.

'Don't worry,' Clare told me.

'I worry all the time,' I replied.

'You know I'll always support you,' she said. 'I believe you absolutely. And I won't leave you either. I think of you all day, every day.'

I returned to my cell in a daze, thinking of her, thrilled that she still believed and trusted in me, but fearful that it would be almost impossible for her to wait for me if my case did, in fact, take two years to come to court. Back in my cell, however, I became morose and tearful once more. Sometimes I became suicidal, afraid that Clare would leave me and that I would be found guilty and probably have to serve 14 years or more in jail. Those thoughts terrified me and, quite often, I knew that would be unbearable. The panic attacks would return after every visit and I would want to scream and cry and smash my head against the wall of the cell, anything, in fact, to relieve the boredom and the depressing, dark thoughts going through my head.

The only way I managed to keep my sanity was thinking of the next visit and working out in the cell. I would do press-ups and sit-ups, which I hoped not only kept my mind on an even keel but would somehow get rid of the natural aggression surging through my body. I had, until then, led a very active, physical life and now, cooped up in the tiny cell, the frustration would become too much and another panic attack would hit me. God, it was awful. During my single hour in the small exercise yard, I would jog around the perimeter and do press-ups and sit-ups, anything to keep my muscles toned and my mind alert.

Those 'closed' visits, as they were called, continued for three months. And for every visit the same precautions were taken by the prison authorities. What annoyed me was the fact that these visits were scheduled to last 45 minutes, but because of the strict precautions insisted upon by the authorities it meant that, in fact, I only spent about 15 minutes with my visitor. I asked whether the visits could be extended, but this was refused.

'Why?' I asked. 'I have been told that I am allowed 45 minutes with a visitor.'

'Bad luck,' was the usual reply.

And after almost six months, my lawyer said he would ask a court to grant me bail, though he had very little hope that would be granted. But others arrested at the same time had been granted bail, and he hoped the authorities would therefore be unable to keep me in jail. It worked. One minute I faced months on end in solitary confinement, the next I was a free man. My parents had agreed to put up their home as security against me absconding.

I was in my cell waiting to hear the outcome of the bail application, when I heard the footsteps of a prison officer outside. I heard him open the cell door, convinced he would tell me my application had been thrown out and I feared another terrifying panic attack.

'Get your stuff together,' was all he said.

'Get lost,' I said, 'you're not winding me up like that.'

'You can go,' he said.

'Bullshit,' I replied.

'It's up to you,' he said. 'I'll leave your cell door open and when you're ready just leave.'

He took out the key and left the door wide open. I walked to the door and looked out, wondering if this was some sort of trick. The place was empty and I could hear his footsteps disappearing. It was at that moment that I fully realised I was a free man. I began to shake like a leaf.

I could hardly believe what he had told me. I could hardly control my thoughts or take in the fact that I was now a free man. I can hardly recall what happened that day but I phoned my parents and told them the fantastic news. Clare was away and I couldn't contact her. Then I found myself out of the jail and I was nervous and shaking as I walked through the gates and to freedom.

Across the road from the jail was a pub, and I walked in and asked for a pint of Guinness. I was trembling, my nerves on edge, barely able to accept that I was tasting freedom.

'Just out?' the landlord asked.

'Yeah,' I replied, somewhat startled by the question.

I arrived home and looked around the house, and my parents hugged me and welcomed me and I felt as though I was in a daze.

I went to my room, changed into my own clothes and packed a rucksack. Then I went out to the garage and found my bicycle and pumped up the tyres. I said 'goodbye' to my parents, telling them I had to get away and savour my freedom. I took off, cycling into the countryside alone, looking at the trees that were losing their leaves, the woods and the rolling fields. I listened to the birds and watched the clouds in the sky, appreciating for the first time in my life the beauty of nature and the sanctity of freedom. Tears of joy came into my eyes and I couldn't stop them. I spent two days cycling around Somerset, at one moment thrilled at being free, the next concerned and worried that one day I might have to return to the horror of solitary confinement.

But I didn't.

The court case was in January 1999. It was thrown out of court. There was never even a trial. Legal arguments took place in court, at the end of which I had no case to answer. My nightmare was at an end, and my new life was just beginning.